MW01003153

# Tales from the
# MARQUETTE
# HARDWOOD

## Tom Pipines
### and
## Mike Neufeldt

www.SportsPublishingLLC.com

ISBN: 1-58261-264-1

© 2005 by Tom Pipines and Mike Neufeldt

All rights reserved. Except for use in a review, the reproduction or utilization of this work in any form or by any electronic, mechanical, or other means, now known or hereafter invented, including xerography, photocopying, and recording, and in any information storage and retrieval system, is forbidden without the written permission of the publisher.

Publishers: Peter L. Bannon and Joseph J. Bannon Sr.
Senior managing editor: Susan M. Moyer
Acquisitions editor: Mike Pearson
Developmental editor: Elisa Bock Laird
Art director: K. Jeffrey Higgerson
Dust jacket design: Dustin Hubbart
Interior layout: Kathryn R. Holleman
Photo editor: Erin Linden-Levy
Media and promotions managers: Letha Caudill (regional),
    Randy Fouts (national), Maurey Williamson (print)

Printed in the United States of America

Sports Publishing L.L.C.
804 North Neil Street
Champaign, IL 61820

Phone: 1-877-424-2665
Fax: 217-363-2073
www.SportsPublishingLLC.com

*From one coauthor to another:*

Mike,

*Thanks for being such an inspiration and great friend all these years. Your humility and courage make you a true hero in my eyes. This book would never have come to fruition without you.*

*Sincerely,*
*Tom*

# Contents

FOREWORD . . . . . . . . . . . . . . . . . . . . . . . . . . . . . . . . . vii

PREFACE . . . . . . . . . . . . . . . . . . . . . . . . . . . . . . . . . . . xi

ACKNOWLEDGMENTS . . . . . . . . . . . . . . . . . . . . . . . . . . xiii

CHAPTER 1: **The 1977 Championship Season** . . . . . . . . . . . . . . . . . . . . . . 1

CHAPTER 2: **Bill Raftery** . . . . . . . . . . . . . . . . . . 17

CHAPTER 3: **Henry "Hank" Raymonds** . . . . 21

CHAPTER 4: **Glenn "Doc" Rivers** . . . . . . . . . . . 31

CHAPTER 5: **Rick Majerus** . . . . . . . . . . . . . . . . . . 39

CHAPTER 6: **Bob Dukiet** . . . . . . . . . . . . . . . . . . . 55

CHAPTER 7: **Tony Smith** . . . . . . . . . . . . . . . . . . . 63

CHAPTER 8: **Kevin O'Neill** . . . . . . . . . . . . . . . . . 71

CHAPTER 9: **Jim McIlvaine** . . . . . . . . . . . . . . . . . 79

CHAPTER 10: **Mike Deane** . . . . . . . . . . . . . . . . . . . 97

CHAPTER 11: **Tom Crean** . . . . . . . . . . . . . . . . . . . 109

CHAPTER 12: **Dwyane Wade** . . . . . . . . . . . . . . . . 133

CHAPTER 13: **Travis Diener** . . . . . . . . . . . . . . . . . 143

CHAPTER 14: **The Voices of Marquette** . . . . . 149

CHAPTER 15: **Jim Langenkamp** . . . . . . . . . . . . . 165

CHAPTER 16: **Bill Cords** . . . . . . . . . . . . . . . . . . . . 171

# Foreword

I t was indeed an honor for me to be a principal in as well as to offer my perspective on this terrific book by Tom Pipines and Mike Neufeldt. It certainly took me down memory lane, which, when it comes to Marquette, is one of my favorite addresses. I still have some regret that when the baton was passed to me, I couldn't have carried it going faster and further. However, I was very fortunate to be part of the race, particularly when Al McGuire and Hank Raymonds were at the controls.

I felt that it was certainly a privilege to be an aspiring young coach in those early years. My Marquette experience helped me to become a much better coach and to have very successful stints at both Ball State and the University of Utah.

I can't begin to tell you as a former Warrior how much you'll enjoy this visit to the past, with its insightful interviews offered by everyone from Raymonds through Tom Crean, the exception being Bob Dukiet. Bob would have enjoyed chronicling his legacy in this book as well, because it would have been treated with great fairness above all else by the authors. It's a shame that Bob couldn't stop playing "Moon River" long enough to have enjoyed the engaging style and heartfelt passion that these two authors bring to bear on the Marquette basketball history.

Alumni everywhere, even Hilltoppers, will very much celebrate, as well as commiserate over, the tremendous highs of Marquette basketball as experienced during the course of many of our lifetimes. Imagine being privy to the events and stories encompassing three Final Fours and giving rise to so many great players, almost all of whom are exemplary human beings in the conduct of their lives. However, these stories take you through the Bo Ellises, Butchie Lees, Doc Riverses, Tony Smiths, and Brian Brunkhorsts (no, that's not a sausage), and it helps you to understand why guys like Earl Tatum, Marc Marotta, Bill Neary, and company are still so much a part of the fabric that makes up the Golden Eagles family, as well as the greater Milwaukee community.

Take this book home and give it to somebody who loves Marquette like you do. Hell, give it to a Badgers fan for that matter, and he can see that they're just on the cusp of trying to approximate what is the Warrior Legend, the Golden Eagles legacy. This storied past encompasses as an eclectic a group of coaches as there may have been at any program through the course of basketball in the 20th and early 21st centuries.

Can you imagine a more diverse group of coaches? McGuire made the Fellowship of Christian Athletes all-opponent team almost every year, and Hank made Mass almost every day. Dukiet wanted to play "Ring out a Hoya," Deane harbored a desire to sing "Ring out a Hoya," and O'Neill lived a life where he *did* "Ring out a Hoya" late into the night. Probably no one ahoy-ed more after a win than O'Neill, and no one agonized more after a loss than me. Some of these guys may have enjoyed the "Highlife," and yes, I am talking about a Miller brew after wins *or* losses. I sequestered myself in the film room, much as Crean does, with a bowl of Real Chili. Luckily, Blonde was there to mix it up, even for the carry out.

This book is going to "slow-mo" some terrific memories and to provide fast-break insight for you into some aspects of the rich Marquette tradition that you haven't been exposed to before. I have sat down with these authors for hours on end and given them a couple of stories, or peeks into the past, that I have not revealed to anyone. I have so much respect for Tom and Mike's journalistic integrity and their investigatory efforts, as well as for their desire to "get it right!" This dynamic duo presents a fair and balanced look on the Warriors tradition that means so much to all of us.

On many occasions, I was asked to speak in Al's stead. So please let me take some poetic license, but without hyperbole, to let you know now that if the revered coach were here today, he would so much enjoy this book and say, "Buy it gang, it's a keeper read!" He would love its intellectual honesty. The genuineness and gemütlichkeit that permeate the pages of this book speak to the authenticity of Raymonds and McGuire.

Al himself could not offer a better perspective on the keepers of the flame: Dukiet, O'Neill, Deane, and Crean. And yes, those four I put into rhythmic rhyme, but only because—in deference to the great coach himself—he would have enjoyed and regaled in the stories of all of his successors who had to chase that brass ring, live in that shadow, and try to "give 'em hell."

It wasn't seashells and balloons for very many of us. We all had our day in the sun, but none of us stood the test of time. Hank did a great job leaving me with a superb program, but we were rendered impotent by the vagaries of being an independent without affiliation when the Big East came into play. Then, of course, the state was bereft of talent, and I was fortunate to get Tony Smith and leave him for Dukiet.

Kevin O'Neill brought Marquette back into the local recruiting picture. He blitzed the Badgers. However, Crean has done the best job of recruiting since those early days in the mid-1970s when Marquette was at the top of almost every city kid's list, because of its commitment to what in those days was the biggest dream of all: getting that piece of paper.

All of us did it in a different way. The methodology was varied, diverse, yet still very much degree oriented. The recruiting tactics, and where we tried to locate players, took us down different paths. Yet, each of us felt the frustration of succeeding a living legend, so much so that O'Neill and I left of our own volition.

It looks like I have ventured off on a McGuire-like tangent. But let me return to the here and now of how wonderfully portrayed this whole ceramic is: *Tales from the Marquette Hardwood* is characterized by its lack of embellishment or hyperbole and is written with striking realism, augmented by anecdote. This is one Marquette read that you won't want to put down.

At the risk of being redundant, I hope you enjoy this book as much as I have. It brought back the seashells, the balloons, and also the heartaches associated with Al having hung the moon for the

Warriors faithful! Some of the memories at the time were not pleasant, but all are factual, heartfelt, and necessary, in order to convey an accurate portrayal of events past. You discover what it is that a dynasty entails. Its dreams, its aspirations, its stars and role players, and its past and present. They're all here on display in a way that has not quite been depicted as such until this time.

I can still see it in my mind's eye to this very day, vivid, dramatic, and theatrical. William Geischeker brings in the band. The faithful rise. The ROTC honor guard comes on the court. Bob Weingardt puts that cigarette down, and Doc Ike starts shakin' on the end of the bench. The national anthem ends, and someone yells out, "Give 'em hell, Al!"

That's what Tom and Mike have done in this book. They've given hell to Al and everyone else. And you'll enjoy—wishing you were there to hear it yet again, yell it again, or understand what it is that "Give 'em hell, Al!" has meant to so many, as we go Crean-ing into that great unknown of the Big East. We all are wanting to bring along the old Warrior, the young Golden Eagle, and blend them into a Big East Conference title gold rush. That is what this book does. It gives us a gold rush of all of our emotions past and present, with possibilities of new ones for you to enjoy.

Hope I'm there late at night sitting next to you with Real Chili, so that we can regale each other with the new stories, old anecdotes, and factual first-person accounts, so wonderfully expressed in this great legacy for all of us to enjoy as we embark upon another season of Marquette basketball.

**—Rick Majerus**

# Preface

## A Tribute to Those Who Came Before

This book covers the period in Marquette basketball history from the MU godfather—Al McGuire—to current coach Tom Crean. Although I (Tom Pipines) have been blessed to be a sportscaster in Milwaukee for quite some time (more than 23 years), even I don't go back to the 1916-1917 season (though that would come as a surprise to some)!

That year, coach Ralph Risch led Marquette to an 8-3 record. Wins came against the likes of Whitewater Normal, Milwaukee Normal, and Oshkosh Normal. Leading scorer Al Delmore averaged a robust 7.3 points per game!

Jack Ryan took the reigns for the 1917-1918 and 1919-1920 seasons. They didn't play any games during the 1918-1919 campaign because of World War I.

Frank Murray took over in 1920-1921; the Murray era stretched through the 1928-1929 season. Murray compiled a fine 94-73 record. Cord Lipe coached in 1929-1930.

Then came Bill Chandler. His leadership lasted 21 seasons, eight more than McGuire, who stands second in longevity with 13. Chandler compiled a record of 193-198. His granddaughter Nancy Chandler, a big-time sports buff in her own right, was a prominent anchor/reporter in the Milwaukee market during the 1980s and 1990s.

Tex Winter, universally respected in the college and pro game, coached from 1951 to 1953. His Marquette team won the 1952 National Catholic Tournament Championship.

Jack Nagle led the way from 1953 to 1958. He was followed by Eddie Hickey from 1958 to 1964. Then came a man named Al.

Our hats are off to the coaches who brought Marquette basketball to that point.

But nobody argues that McGuire set the standard—putting Marquette and Milwaukee on the college basketball map with that magical 1977 season—his last as Warriors coach.

# Acknowledgments

W e would like to thank the individuals who graciously shared their Marquette memories. Without their help, this book would not be possible.

Bill Cords, Tom Crean, Mike Deane, Travis Diener, Dr. Jim Langenkamp, Rick Majerus, Jim McIlvaine, Kevin O'Neill, Bill Raftery, Henry "Hank" Raymonds, Glenn "Doc" Rivers, Clyde Rusk, Tony Smith, George Thompson, Steve "The Homer" True, and Dwyane Wade.

In addition, we want to thank:

• Mike Broeker, Marquette University assistant athletics director—media relations; Marquette University Intercollegiate Athletics Department; and the Marquette University Department of Special Collections and University Archives;

• WITI FOX 6 Sports archives; WITI FOX 6 art department; and

• Carol Neufeldt for her editing.

## Media Citations

*Milwaukee Journal Sentinel, New York Post,* WITI FOX 6 Sports Archives, and *USA Today*

# Chapter 1

# The 1977 Championship Season

A l McGuire was the ninth head coach in Marquette University basketball annals. He was by far the most successful. In 13 seasons (1964-1977) at the helm of the Warriors, the incomparable Irishman posted a record of 295 wins, compared with just 80 losses, for a winning percentage of .787. Under McGuire, the Warriors made 11 postseason appearances. They won 27 of 37 tournament games, including one NIT championship. But McGuire's legacy will forever be linked to the magical run to the 1977 NCAA championship in his final season as coach.

## An Unexpected Announcement

"The biggest upset ever in the history of the NCAA was Marquette winning the NCAA. Don't you remember? We were the last team invited," Al McGuire joked during the 1977 season.

Al McGuire's remarkable run to the 1977 NCAA championship in his final season as Marquette coach was unlikely, to say the least. Actually, the journey to the Omni in Atlanta was expected—before the season began. After losing to eventual champion Indiana the year before, McGuire's Warriors were ranked No. 1 in the nation by UPI and No. 2 by the AP. They jumped out to a 4-0 start before Al shocked his players and Marquette fans. On December 17, 1976,

Bo Ellis was the captain of the Warriors' NCAA championship team.

*From the Marquette University Department of Special Collections and University Archives*

McGuire announced that he was resigning as coach effective at the end of the season.

Bo Ellis: "At first, we knew something was wrong when Coach had us gather together at the Times Building for lunch. He never did anything like that."

Jerome Whitehead: "I got a strange feeling that something normal wasn't about to take place, because normally, if we have a meeting like that, it's not because it's a birthday party. So I got the sense that something uneasy was about to take place. I just didn't know what it was."

McGuire said that after 26 years in the coaching business, he was looking for a change. He had accepted an offer from Medalist Industries—a Milwaukee-based firm.

Butch Lee: "I don't think nobody expected that, and we were all pretty sad at the time."

Ulice Payne: "I think that when Coach announced his retirement, that did put a little extra juice in it, which may have caused some problems for us. I think we were playing for something other than ourselves. Coach always told us to play for ourselves."

Apparently, that was the case, because Al's Warriors seemed to lose focus. They lost two games before Christmas.

Payne: "It did hit us at that point, and so we noticed a difference in Coach, too. I think that Coach began to coach. Historically, he would allow Hank Raymonds or Rick Majerus to do all the things, but we noticed that he was at the practices when they started. He talked about what to do on the court, when, historically, he didn't do much of that until game time. And so we started to see a change in him, and that affected us as well."

Majerus: "I have vivid, vivid memories of [the 1977 season]. I have memories of where I was talking to the team, when Al told me he was going to quit. It was one of the few days where he sat the team down. I could put the benches where they were today.

"He just said, 'Look, this is going to be my last year.'

"He did this in October and November. That kind of cast a pall over the whole season. That was a tough meeting. At that point it was, 'Is Hank going to succeed him? Should he succeed him? Was Al a lame duck coach?' Sure he was. That was kind of a tough situation. We thought we were going to be good, but I think Al felt we had our best chance to win it in 1974. Al thought, too, that the referees had a prejudice against him come tournament time. The reason was that he was kind of arrogant and obnoxious, and he talked about them at tournament time. I think he felt, too, that the NCAA hierarchy didn't want a guy like him, because he had shunned the NCAA Tournament bid in 1970 and went to the NIT.

"He would blast Walter Beyers [then NCAA Tournament head] on occasion. We thought we had a good team; we thought we had a tournament team, but nobody thought that team was going to go on and win a national championship!"

## Regular Season

Raymonds and McGuire were the perfect mix. Raymonds was the Xs and Os guy, brilliant at pregame preparation. McGuire was the master motivator, possessing strong people skills and bench coach ability.

"I'm trying to make a person take one more step than he wants to," McGuire told reporters during the season. "I'm trying to have him dig deep down into his gut. These types of things are done in my world by violence—verbal violence. The only thing I can say is I treated them all the same. It was my way of trying to get out what God had put in them. These fellas, the talented ones, the Michael Angelos, the talent was in the crib. But it has to come out. It's a mortal sin if you don't get it out of a person. My way of doing it is to hammer physically and verbally hammer."

Payne: "Coach McGuire was always tough; he was tough on the waiter; he was tough on the bus driver; he was tough on everybody."

Robert Byrd: "When Coach said early that he was gonna leave, it became more of a motivation for the team, as well as everybody that was associated. Let's win this thing. His back was to the wall, and when his back was to the wall, he was very, very competitive.

You didn't want to fight with him. He's always gonna come out smellin' like a rose when his back was to the wall."

Marquette bounced back, running off 10 straight wins before stalling. The Warriors dropped four of their next six, including setbacks in each of the final three home games of McGuire's career. Their tournament hopes were in limbo. There was the Valentine's Day heartbreaker against DePaul. The Blue Demons won a double-overtime thriller. Two days later, Dick Vitale's Detroit team visited MECCA Arena. Dennis Boyd buried a jumper to lift the Titans to a 64-63 win. At 16-5, Marquette's tournament hopes were fading.

"No way, no way," McGuire said then. "If you can't win at home, how ya gonna win on the road?"

Before McGuire's final game at home, he was honored with gifts as a thank you for 13 seasons. Wichita State won that final game in Milwaukee. Bo Ellis was hit with two second-half technical fouls. He'd been punched by a Wichita State player. Marquette lost by 11.

Payne: "Coach cried when we lost that last home game, and they booed him as we walked out. He couldn't believe that we would leave the Milwaukee arena losing three in a row."

Majerus: "The most vivid memory to me is Al and the team getting booed the last game at home when we lost to Wichita State. The talk shows weren't as prevalent in those days. There was a great guy on the radio locally. He was one of the finest human beings you'd ever know. His name was Jack Baker. Even Jack had a disparaging comment, not mean spirited at all, but he said that Al shouldn't have done it this way. It was probably time for him to go, because Al had lost interest in the game. He admitted he'd lost interest in the game. Al got worn out. We had a vice president of student affairs named Jim Scott, who would memo you to death. They were always worried about what he was making and what he was doing in the offseason. That would weigh on Al. They got into these paper memo wars. Hank [Raymonds] was kind of an intermediary. There was always kind of a sadness in the offices because of budgets, BS stuff, and vacations; they wanted him to chart his vacation days. They got wrapped up in this, and that sent Al out the door as quick as anything.

"Then, we got booed off of the court. Four weeks later, 10,000, 20,000 people—these same people who I had seen, who had spoken so badly of Al and Hank and the team, and who were so disillusioned—were now our newest best friends the night we won our national championship. That's the thing that stuck with me. I remember giving my dad my NCAA watch that night. I remember how proud he was. I remember my mom and dad being there."

Raymonds: "Ya lose three in a row at home; ya gotta play five more games on the road! Ya don't even know if you're going to a tournament!"

## A Tournament Bid

Suddenly, Marquette became "Road Warriors." They won at Wisconsin, Virginia Tech, and Tulane. A win at Creighton marked the 200th victory of McGuire's MU career. The tournament bid came—during the Michigan game. McGuire's swansong would feature a trip to the NCAA's field of 32. Coach finally changed his lucky suit at halftime in Ann Arbor.

"At halftime they're all hugging each other," McGuire said after the game, "and they're all sweating, and I got pretty good clothes on!"

Payne: "We were winning at halftime. We got an announcement that we were in the tournament; we lost the game. We lost our concentration; we started thinking about other things again, more for Coach than for us; and we lost the game."

Bernard Toone: "We were really happy that we got the tournament bid, and we were gonna play like the No. 1 team people ranked us to be at the beginning of the season."

"Well it's one game at a time, but it's an opportunity," McGuire said to reporters in 1977. "You're one of 32 teams, and I'd like to thank the ballplayers and the coaching staff for doing it. It was kind of a bad week there, two or three weeks ago. It was like building

Edsels, and we kind of ended up in the minus pool. But they regrouped and did it. I would like to have gotten the momentum from this game and gone into Omaha next week. But ya know, I shouldn't say this, 'cuz it'll come back to me, but not many people are so lucky to go to Omaha twice in one week!"

Payne: "It wasn't until then that we saw all the media come around. We saw stories all the time, and he did interviews. But it wasn't until the last week after February that we started to realize, 'Ya know what, these *are* the last interviews!'"

"The whole year's been a tremendous drain on me," McGuire confessed then. "I really think that it's been like four years this one year. So I'm just trying to leave clean, and I hope that the ball goes in, and we can take Marquette down to Atlanta and be in the Final Four."

## The Tournament

After losing in the 1976 tournament, McGuire swore he wouldn't coach in it again. But the coach said he was back by popular demand, thanks to a petition being passed around an Irish bar by his mom, and someone named "Monsignor Godblessyou!" McGuire even donned his lucky suit for the entire tourney!

And so the tourney's trail began with 32 teams. It would take five victories to bring home a championship. The magical run began at the Civic Center in Omaha, Nebraska.

Raymonds: "The first game was Cincinnati. And we had lost to Cincinnati by one point in the last minute on a very controversial call at their place. And we had to play them in Omaha."

Majerus: "Al put [Bernard] Toone in the game. He hated Toone because Toone was a little bit arrogant, cocky. He was one of those media myths. He didn't have a good work ethic; he was immature. He was kind of a party guy. Al got upset with all that—not that some of the other guys weren't party guys. Everyone in college had a party life, but you had to compartmentalize it. But Toone had the glove compartment for academics, and the rest of the car was for parties! There wasn't much left for basketball.

"Anyway, we were playing Cincinnati in Omaha. Al took Toone out of the game for a bad shot.

"Toone said to him, '**** you.'

"We came in at halftime. Al couldn't let it go. He went underneath Toone's chin, and he started saying something to him. He gave him the finger, and then he slapped him.

"Then Toone got up, and Toone didn't want any part of Al. That was good, because if he had, there would have been some kind of brawl in the locker room. All I remember is [trainer Bob] Weingardt got in and got his hand hurt somehow, and I grabbed Toone. I took Toone, and I lifted him up.

"We went outside the locker room. In those days, there was like a concession stand press area.

"So the media guys said, 'What are you doing out here?'

"I say, 'I'm just stretching Bernard.' Some BS like that.

"I said to Toone, 'You didn't mean that when you said that to him, and he didn't mean it to you.'

"He came back in. They didn't say a word to each other. Hank tried to get some semblance of order relative to the game. Al knew he had lost it, but we went out in the second half. It was one of those things where they got banded together by the adversity of the situation. Everyone played their asses off. In Toone's defense, he handled it pretty well. After the game, we were all in there hugging each other! Both guys were wrong; both guys never said anything.

Gary Rosenberger: "That was where the rubber met the road, ya know? We're up six to eight points against Cincinnati. Bernard Toone made a couple mistakes boxing out a guy; we had an altercation at halftime, coaches against players, kind of the WWF in today's world. And at the end of the halftime, Bernard was crying. Bo was saying, 'Let's get 'em in the second half.' Bernard had a great second half, and we buried Cincinnati, and I think that was the trampoline that took us to the national title."

Raymonds: "We went on to Kansas State. In my mind, my opinion, that was the best team we played, well-coached, not big. They played a zone against us. We couldn't do much of anything. Al gets a technical. He leaned over to me and said, 'Hank, if we lose this game, I'm finished for life.' The kid who went in the game, Jim Dudley, hit a turnaround, and we won by one."

Majerus: "The game that was even more difficult to win was the game against the great [Kansas State] Jack Hartman-coached team. Everyone alludes to the North Carolina–Charlotte game, where we hit the last-second shot. I remember that game in Omaha. I remember walking with Al before that game. It was a dreary, cold spring day in Omaha. He just kept walking and walking. He had started his toy soldier kick then. He was very philosophical, not unlike [Bill] Clinton when the press was on him a bit. Everyone asked Al why he had announced his retirement at that time. He was very sensitive to the situation. He didn't feel appreciated by the administration at Marquette. It was time for him to quit anyway, but it was like a magical moment."

The Warriors met Wake Forest in the regional final. Bernard Toone scored 16 points in the second half. Marquette breezed into the Final Four at the Omni in Atlanta.

## Not Enough Tickets

Majerus: "One of my 'big' jobs in 1977 at the Final Four was Al said, 'Rick, tonight you might have the most important job in the whole arena.'

"'Fine, Coach,' I said. 'Do you want me to chart something?'

"He said, 'You have to get there two hours early and let three guys in the back door, 'cuz we don't have enough tickets!'

"One was a guy named Renee Miller, whom Al did clinics for the United States Air Force. I think Bill Hughes ended up getting scalped tickets. He was our travel agent. He and Al were splitting some of the money that they were scalping tickets on. I can't remember the third guy.

"Can you imagine in this day and age, meeting someone at the back door, opening up the door, and then meeting them at the arena? I brought them into the locker room."

## Final Four

In the semifinals, Marquette faced North Carolina–Charlotte—featuring future pro star Cornbread Maxwell.

Rosenberger: "North Carolina-Charlotte? Who are these guys? We take the floor; both their guards are like six foot three, six foot four, built like Hercules. They've got Cornbread Maxwell and two big, strong forwards. And we're like, 'This is gonna be a physical basketball game.'"

The Warriors led by four at halftime. Maxwell led UNCC back, but he missed a key free throw down the stretch. The game was tied 49-49 with three seconds left; Marquette had the ball; a timeout was called.

Lee: "Ya know, Al told me to hold on a minute, and he came down to the other end of the court to try and check the clock. There's no way we could have hit that [overhead scoreboard if we had thrown a full-court pass]!"

Ellis: "The play was initially supposed to be thrown to me, and I was supposed to turn around and try to shoot it. Butch really overthrew his receiver, because I was the receiver, but I'm glad he did!"

Whitehead: "It's amazing how destiny has its little twist. I remember Butch throwing the ball, and I remember Bo reaching for it. It lightly hit off his fingertips, and as it did, it made a little trajectory over our heads right there in front. I was like, 'Just take it in.' And so I was gonna go in and dunk it, and the guy Maxwell came in and fouled me, and it went in."

Ellis: "And all I could remember was when Jerome caught it, turned, and got it off, and the ball bounced around the rim, and I jumped about [six feet in the air]."

Payne: "And we hoped they were going to count it, and for a while there, there was so much emotion. The question was did Jerome tap it in in time."

Raymonds: "And now, we gotta go over to the table, and the middle official pushes everybody out of the way and tells the timer, 'Now take your time. I want you to think. Did that ball leave his hand before you pressed that button?' And the guy says, 'Yes,' and so we win."

Whitehead: "That was really an indication—if we could get that far and if we could win. I didn't want to say it was a sign that we're going all the way."

"There's a rhythm to basketball like there is to life," McGuire said during the 1977 season, "and you must stay within your own rhythm. If you play someone else's rhythm, you'll end up in tap city."

Jim Boylan: "Any kids who were out there—I'm sure that they were thinking after they watched the Marquette game that they're probably going to go out to the playgrounds and they're going to shoot jump shots and win the game, ya know. You think about it all the time. You'd sit in your room and think about the last three seconds ticking off and you're in the national championship. I'd just think what it would be like to be the national champs, ya know, and I wanted to have that feeling."

## Championship Night

March 28, 1977, Marquette faces North Carolina. Coach McGuire faces good friend Dean Smith, hoping for a storybook ending to his career.

Payne: "I think for the players, it was one of those things where we may not get back here, and now it's Coach's last game. This is *really* Coach's last game! I think the *Atlanta Constitution* and all the media, it was again, this is Coach's last game, as opposed to the NCAA championship. I think that's where the motivation really started out, 'cuz we realized this is the last 40 minutes we have with Coach."

Rosenberger: "And I think at that point in time, it would have taken an awesome game by North Carolina to beat Marquette that night. We were just in a frame of mind that it's a do-or-die deal. This is Coach's last game, 26 years of coaching; we know it's over; this is the last game. We're leaving it all out on the court."

For the first 20 minutes, the Warriors were unstoppable. Behind Butch Lee's 15 points, McGuire's men took a 12-point lead into halftime, but Dean Smith's Tar Heels roared back to take a lead of their own. That's when Smith went to his famous Four Corners offense. The idea was to eat up the clock.

Raymonds: "For once, they went into it at the wrong time. They had momentum; they were playing well; they came from 12 points behind. They were moving, and then they got up by two. And they went into the Four Corners, and we didn't care if they held onto the ball out there. We just dropped back, more or less, like a combination man and zone. As a result, the clock kept moving, and close games are our bread and butter. We didn't care."

The rest, as they say, is history. The Warriors went into a Four Corners style of their own. Jim Boylan hit the go-ahead basket. When the final buzzer sounded, Marquette had a 67-59 victory— and the national crown!

Majerus: "In the North Carolina game, when we were playing for the national championship, we were bound and determined to play man-to-man. We were a good man-to-man team because Al held them accountable. He was a much better coach and tactician than he gave himself credit for. He had that self-deprecating sense of humor; he really knew what was going on. Hank was a great tactician, too. Together they were a great team, because neither one would let egos get in the way. Anyway, we always zoned the end out-of-bounds play. For years in McGuire's career he said, 'It's stupid to play man-to-man on end outs.' I played man-to-man my whole career on end outs because there was almost like a father/son rivalry there. So we play this 2-3 zone. Carolina had about two or three

Following their NCAA championship victory, coach Al McGuire and the Warriors met President Jimmy Carter. *From the Marquette University Department of Special Collections and University Archives*

inbounds plays. He saw there was trouble there. Al was a great bench coach in terms of recognizing situations in games. He saw that they struggled, and they weren't in any way prepared to play against our zone because we didn't zone. He stayed with the zone, and that helped. When they didn't come out of the Four Corners, that was a big plus. Everyone alludes to that as a strategic downfall of Carolina and a great asset for us. Al wasn't afraid to take chances. He didn't play by the numbers. He was exploratory in games. He didn't get wrapped up in, "It's my way or the highway, or this is the way we're going to win." He was a system coach, but he was also a personnel coach. He was a seat-of-the-pants adjustment guy, and I would say 90 percent of the time he was right. He wasn't afraid to make mistakes. He wasn't afraid to be wrong. Sometimes as coaches, we all play it too conventionally. That's what made him good, too.

"The one thing I remember, too, in the national championship when we won, Al had a longtime friend, Normie Oaks, out of New York. He and Normie were really close. Normie was a good guy, and he really idolized Al. He really helped spearhead Al into the Hall of Fame. I'll never forget when he came up to Al on the court in the national championship after we had won.

"He said, 'Al, do you know what this means? Do you know what this means?'

"Normie was a basketball purest, a friend of Dickie McGuire [Al's brother], and a great player in his own right back in New York collegially and from the old Rockaway Beach days [Al's hometown]. He was hoping that Al was going to say, 'This is the realization of all my basketball dreams.'

"Al said, 'Ten years of speaking engagements!'"

Raymonds: "All I remember is sittin' on that bench, and when it was over, seein' old tough guy breakin' up and crying!"

McGuire's tears were discussed in the postgame news conference. McGuire was asked why he went to the locker room before coming back out.

"I wanted to compose myself," he explained to the press. "I cried. I'm not ashamed to cry. I just don't like to do it in front of people."

Whitehead: "It was good to see Coach crying, 'cuz when we were in college, he used to holler so much. So it was like, oh, so you do have an emotional side; you just hide it!"

Payne: "Again, it seems like yesterday, 'cuz I can remember seeing Coach cry, one more time. So we'd seen the tough guy cry in the Milwaukee Arena, the last home game. We didn't think we were going to the tournament; he didn't either. Now, we saw him cry, being so happy, after the tournament."

Rosenberger: "I'll never forget, standing at halfcourt at the Omni in Atlanta, cutting down the nets saying, 'This is what all the playground games were for, and it all seems worth it.'"

"I remember Bo [Ellis] going through the top of the rim with the backboard," McGuire told reporters, "and I just remember everybody holding each other. And that's my thoughts, and those thoughts will be with me, until I cash in …. Why me, ya know, all the wet jocks and the socks, driving the car at Belmont Abbey with the kids, that type of stuff … freshman coaching at Dartmouth, and thinking of all the PALs and the CYOs. All the odors of the locker rooms, that type of stuff, all the fights in the different gyms. I used to be a real obnoxious person. I guess I still am, but I was really then. The wildness of it all and just have your team reach the peak first."

# CHAPTER 2

# Bill Raftery

Bill Raftery has been an analyst for CBS Sports's college basketball coverage for over 20 years. Raftery was head coach of Seton Hall University from 1970 to 1982. He led the Pirates to a 154-141 record during his tenure. Raftery and Al McGuire broadcast college basketball games together for CBS Sports, and he has many fond memories of McGuire.

## Selling Marquette

Raftery: "Anybody of that ilk—a Hank Iba, a Bob Knight—you're in that area where the comparisons are going to be there. I think that's what Al McGuire had established at Marquette. There was probably a false sense of accomplishment in the Milwaukee and Marquette communities. What you had was a unique style that attracted kids, whether it was a suburban tough kid or an inner-city shooter or just the opposite. He might get a tough inner-city player or a setup shooter from the 'burbs. Al was why they came to Marquette."

## "Spencer Haywood!"

Raftery: "I miss him. I think of him with incidents and situations, some of his insights, his approach to life. I remember being at a function where he was honored. We didn't have a dais. We just had a microphone. Anyway, he sat with my wife. They had prizes and gifts. One of the gifts was if you could name the first hardship player in the NBA. The answer was Spencer Haywood. Nobody knew it. All of a sudden, my wife puts her hand up. My wife didn't know the names of our players [when I coached at Seton Hall]! So, she was called on.

"'Joan?'

"She said, 'Spencer Haywood!'

"Al had whispered the answer to her in her ear. She won two tickets to dinner or something. That was the devil in him."

## A Friend

Raftery: "Tom Crean and I visited Al together when he was sick. It wasn't about him. It was about, 'What are you guys doing? Where ya going?' If you asked him about himself he'd say, 'Hey, they're doing a good job here.' Blah, blah, blah. There was nothing about him. Al was a real coaches' guy when he left coaching. He was the adviser to guys after they'd had a great run in the NCAA Tournament. He tried to help them go about making their positions better. A lot of guys called him about jobs, particularly anybody who was down and out. He was a friend."

## "They Think They're Dancin'!"

Raftery: "What sticks about the last time I saw Al was that he looked better than had been reported—far better. Mentally, he was as sharp as ever. He was more concerned about staph infection than he was about existing difficulties. I remember he told me Rick had been in to see him the day before. He said Majerus brought in about $100 worth of Mexican food!

Al McGuire, Dick Enberg, and Digger Phelps (left to right) share a laugh before a game. *From the Marquette University Department of Special Collections and University Archives*

"'You know me. I'm not going to touch that! Rick ate most of it.'

"As I was leaving, I was walking down the hallway with him, he said to me, 'I'm the youngest guy here.'

"I said, 'No kidding?'

"He said, 'Yeah.'

"At the end of a hallway there was a rec room. A number of patients had a beach ball. They had the ball in the air. Now they were all older. I looked in to the right. We turned to the elevator, which would be on our left shoulder. The door opened. Al was going to take me down to the first floor, so I could go. We both sort of looked in at the beach ball in the air.

"Al turns to me and he says, 'They think they're dancin'!'

"We were like two schoolboys, giggling as we got on to the elevator. Under the circumstance, you wouldn't have thought that we'd be laughing! That was the last time I was with him. He had said, 'I'm not good.'"

## It Came from the Heart

Raftery: "Regrettably, I couldn't get a plane in from Vancouver in time to make the funeral. Having said that, he's one of the guys I remember in my prayers. Al was a great friend to me. With his passing, the uniqueness of the profession is gone. His natural insight; there's no baloney. What he said came from the heart ... I think he was a far different man than the people knew at Marquette, the last 20 years of his life. He had left his competitive niche, although he was still competitive. One of his enjoyments in life was people. The young people where he worked at CBS just couldn't believe it. He treated these intern types as though they were executive producers. It was a thrill for everybody at CBS to work with this guy."

## Positively Influenced

Raftery: "Tim Ryan [the play-by-play announcer] got the biggest kick out of working with him. It filtered down to the whole gang.

"Al McGuire may not have come across as the most religious man. In the latter days of his life, this Catholic from the streets of New York joked that life was good because 'he was giving his confession to a deaf priest!' But he was spiritual in the way he cared for, and positively influenced, all the people fortunate enough to come across his path. This was never more evident than when Al faced his final days."

# CHAPTER 3

# Henry "Hank" Raymonds

No book about Marquette basketball would be complete without a good portion being devoted to Hank Raymonds. His relationship with Coach McGuire was extraordinary.

## Hank, Meet Al (and Vice Versa)

The two first became acquainted when Hank was coaching Christian Brothers College (now University) in Memphis. He went up against Al's Belmont Abbey Squad, from North Carolina.

Raymonds: "I scheduled Al the year before I left. We paid them $700 to come down and play us. Knowing Al, he probably put the money in his pocket! In the meantime, I left for Milwaukee to join my old coach Eddie Hickey [at Marquette]. The team I had left behind beat 'em by 16. [Al] made 'em all walk back to the hotel!

"Now it was between him and me for the job at Marquette. Bob Harlan, the sports information director at the time, called me.

"He said, 'Hank, I guess you didn't get it; they gave it to Al.'

"A little while later the phone rang. It's Al."

(Keep in mind, McGuire and Raymonds had never met. They'd only spoken on the phone.)

Hank Raymonds (left) was Al McGuire's (right) top assistant for 13 seasons. After McGuire retired, Raymonds coached the Warriors for six seasons.
*From the Marquette University Department of Special Collections and University Archives*

"He said, 'I'm sorry ya didn't get it, but I want you to stay with me. We'll knock 'em dead. When I was in Memphis, they called you the Adolph Rupp of Memphis.'

"And he kept his word, never fired me."

That was part of McGuire's genius. He saw in Raymonds the strengths that he didn't have.

## House Hunting

McGuire's trust in Raymonds was such that he wrote a blank check, gave it to Raymonds, and had Raymonds buy a house for him that he and his wife, Pat, had seen and liked, because the McGuires had to be out of town. Coach Raymonds even painted the front door!

It's the same house Pat McGuire lives in to this day!

## Feeling Dejected

There were a couple times when Raymonds thought McGuire would leave Marquette. One time was after a loss to Washington University in St. Louis.

Raymonds: "I think it was his second year. Washington U. beat us. We stayed at the Chase near Forest Park. Al walked all the way through that park by himself. He was really dejected. I think he was ready to try to leave."

## Adding a New Assistant

The two men had mostly a business relationship, but they talked often.

Raymonds: "One day Al said, 'We're not getting any younger, we need somebody to help us.'

"Then I suggested that we take Rick [Majerus]. Rick was on my freshman team. He used to come in every day for hours, and we'd talk basketball. Then he was grammar school coach at St. Sebastian and freshman coach at Marquette High School. So we took Rick."

Of course, Majerus went on to become head coach at Marquette University, after Raymonds. After a successful stint at Ball State, Rick went to Utah, where he became one of the top college coaches in America.

## Pipeline to New York City

As good as that coaching staff became, the players put Marquette basketball on the national map. McGuire and Raymonds developed a pipeline to New York City. They got to know a man through South Carolina coach Frank McGuire (no relation). Mike Tynberg made his living in railroads.

Raymonds: "I used to call him and wake him up at noon. But he knew all the kids, even though he didn't know much about basketball. Mike would tell us about players and talk to them about Marquette."

The pipeline produced the likes of George Thompson, Dean Meminger, and Butch Lee. A basketball nut, Mike Tyneberg helped MU crack into "The Big Apple" and take a big bite out of the talent there.

## The Bumble Bee Uniforms

Any Marquette fan who goes back to the McGuire days remembers the famous "Bumble Bee" uniforms. Marquette was the guinea pig for those uniforms, which was designed by Medalist Industries of Milwaukee. Medalist was putting all of their competitors out of business, because all of the schools wanted that style. The distinctive look lasted until the NCAA rule committee outlawed them. In their wisdom, the members of that committee said that when the players stretched out and jumped up and down, the uniforms created a "psychedelic effect"!

## A Trip to Brazil

Raymonds: "There was the year [1976] we played in Brazil. We represented the United States. Before we went, Al made everybody sign that they wouldn't wanna come home right away. We got to Brazil. We were gonna practice. The circus had just left the night before. There was oil on the floor, and then they put water on the floor to get rid of the oil! [Jerome] Whitehead fractured his wrist, so

Jim Chones is shown here wearing the "Bumble Bee" uniform, which was eventually banned by the NCAA because it created a "psychedelic effect."
*From the Marquette University Department of Special Collections and University Archives*

Hank Raymonds took the reins of the Warriors for a game during their 1976 tournament appearance in Brazil. A trip that Raymonds was happy to return from—alive. *From the Marquette University Department of Special Collections and University Archives*

he was out. Our first opponent is Brazil in São Paulo. The first thing ya know, a guy from Brazil spat on Bill Neary. Neary complained to the official. The official gave Neary a technical. Neary went over; he proceeded to destroy the water cooler on our bench. So I went out to the floor.

"I told the official, 'We're leaving. We're not putting up with this crap! We're goin' back home!'

"The Portuguese official says in broken English, 'Remember what happened to soccer players two years ago?'

"I said, 'Yeah, they were shot! We'll finish the game.'

"We lost. The next day, Al came into the dressing room and said, 'Hank, you coach today. I'll take Pat and [your wife] Ginny, and we'll sit in the stands and watch the game. By the way, if they shoot you, I'll say a prayer for you.'

"We beat Puerto Rico. Then Al came in and said, 'I'm gonna coach again.'

"Then we moved to Rio. We got to the finals. We beat Yugoslavia. They had a helluva team. We played Brazil for the championship. Tom Nissalke, who coached here in the states, was coaching Puerto Rico.

"He said, 'Hank, don't try to win. If you win, you won't get out of here alive!'

"Our kids got fouls on purpose; we lost the game. As soon as the game was over, there were fireworks. They were happy."

## Hank After Al

Humble and subservient, Hank Raymonds was a key element to the McGuire success story. Hank took the reins from Al after the 1977 championship season. He went on to compile the best record in Marquette history over a six-season span (126-50). Raymonds's teams made the postseason all six years. He also served the university as athletic director during that time and beyond.

Hank Raymonds was inducted into the Wisconsin Sports Hall of Fame in 2005.
*From the Marquette University Department of Special Collections and University Archives*

## Hank Today

In October 2005, Raymonds's marvelous career was capped off by his induction to the prestigious Wisconsin Sports Hall of Fame.

Hank Raymonds is the epitome of class and professionalism. He is a huge part of Marquette ahletics. To this day, he remains one of the university's most loyal supporters.

# CHAPTER 4

# Glenn "Doc" Rivers

efore the arrival of Dwyane Wade, Marquette basketball fans
had seen the likes of another superstar Glenn "Doc" Rivers.
The six-foot-four guard from Maywood, Illinois, was a
spectacular leaper and a superb athlete. An All-American, Rivers
went on to have a solid 13-year pro career with the Atlanta Hawks
(where he was an All-Star), Los Angeles Clippers, New York Knicks,
and San Antonio Spurs. He also coached the Orlando Magic and
Boston Celtics.

## Doc

Rivers: "My first memory of Marquette basketball was as a
freshman in high school, actually. I went to the Medalist Basketball
Camp that Al McGuire and Rick Majerus were running. The day I
registered I had on a Dr. J T-shirt. My name is Glenn; everybody
called me Glenn. At the end of the week, the Milwaukee Bucks
came in to put on an exhibition. They only had nine players, and
they needed a 10th. Al McGuire was looking up in the stands. All
the campers were yelling for 'Doc.' I didn't know who 'Doc' was; I
didn't know that was my name!

"Then Rick looked at me and said, 'It's you, "Doc," you!

"Then all the kids started yelling, 'Doc, Doc, Doc!'

Glenn "Doc" Rivers earned All-America honors while at Marquette.

*From the Marquette University Department of Special Collections and University Archives*

"That's how my name was born! For the next three years in high school, I was still Glenn in Maywood, Illinois. But in Milwaukee, I was 'Doc.' And the day I signed to go to Marquette, the Milwaukee papers said, 'Marquette signs Doc Rivers.' The Chicago papers said, 'Marquette signs Glenn Rivers.' Once I got up here, I don't think Glenn was ever used again. That's the day I remember most about Marquette, because of the camps. I just fell in love with the university as a freshman in high school. From that point on, I always envisioned myself playing for Marquette. When that dream came true, it was really important to me, and it was really a big day for me.

"Marquette was my number-one choice. I took six visits. Notre Dame was one, DePaul, Louisville, and Maryland. But Marquette never wavered. It's funny; I never took an official visit to Marquette. I knew I was going there. I remember Rick and Hank [Raymonds] getting nervous, because I didn't take a visit.

"I kept telling them, 'I don't need to take a visit.'

"They kept saying, 'Well you've gone to all their schools.'

"I said, 'Well, I needed to see those schools. I know Marquette.'

"The first day I went there was the day I signed. I had never even seen the campus. I didn't come there for the campus. I came there for Marquette University and Hank Raymonds and Rick Majerus. That's why I came."

## The Raymonds Influence

Rivers: "Hank has influenced me in a lot of ways. As a player, he showed me that there was more than one way to play the game. He knew that I was an athlete. Hank wanted to show me that you don't have to play at a great speed all the time to be a successful basketball player. He was absolutely right. It's funny you ask how he's influenced me as a coach. It's the number-one thing I try to teach my players—to just play at different speeds. Hank harped on that all the time. If you look at our games today, it's part of the reason they've suffered in college and the pros. The kids don't know

Glenn Rivers earned the nickname "Doc" while attending a basketball camp at Marquette. *From the Marquette University Department of Special Collections and University Archives*

different gears and how to play the game. Hank taught that years ago. I always tell him that he was a man ahead of his time."

## Beating the Irish

Rivers: "The Notre Dame shot [a halfcourt buzzer beater that put the Warriors ahead 54-52 of the fifth-ranked Irish on January 10, 1981], obviously, is the memory that I'll never forget. I remember that game; I actually remember the day. It was one of the coldest days on record—like 80 below with wind-chill factor! I remember them holding the ball. They were up, I think, and they held the ball too long. We forced a turnover. Michael Wilson and I tied up one of the Notre Dame players. That's how we got the ball back. I remember getting the inbound pass and letting it go. I told people later, right when it left my hands, I didn't know if it was going in or not, but I knew it had a chance. When it went in, the funniest thing happened: I ran into the locker room. I made the shot. I was so excited; I ran into the locker room. Nobody was there! I stood there for about two minutes. I came back onto the floor. That was when I saw Michael Wilson standing on top of the rim, and I saw everybody celebrating. I told people I almost missed the celebration, because I ran off the floor! That's a memory I'll never forget."

## From Boy to Man

Rivers: "The university made me a man. I came to Marquette because I wanted to be a basketball player. I didn't come for the right reasons. In the middle of my freshman year there was a professor named Dr. Rhodes. He took a liking to me and basically told me that I was going to be a great student by the time I left. He made me come to his house several times in that year to redo papers. I really believe that of all the things that have happened to me in my life, that may have been the most significant. Because without that, I don't think I would have been a coach. I wouldn't have been a broadcaster for sure. I may have been able to be a basketball player. But I wouldn't have gone any further because I would never have focused as hard as I needed to on the education. I tell kids that all the time. The athletics are great. But if you can do that and get the education, then you can do whatever you want to for the rest of your life."

## Coach or Player?

Rivers: "It's easier to be a player—until you have to face Jordan! Obviously, it's harder physically as a player. The toughest thing I'll

"Doc" Rivers was able to mature as a player and as a person while attending Marquette. *From the Marquette University Department of Special Collections and University Archives*

ever do is be a NBA player. I'll say that, but coaching is more time consuming. It takes me back to childhood days when I was a player. I was just completely consumed by it. Coaching's the same way. I love it. It's part of me. I see myself as a guy who coaches for a long time.

"I never had the goal of becoming a coach. I grew up wanting to be a player. I think most coaches grew up wanting to be players who turned into coaches. At the end of my career, Pat Riley had a profound effect on me as a coach. He coached me when I played for New York. That was when I started thinking that I'd like to do that someday. He did it with so much passion and so much love. I thought, if I can coach that way, I can be successful.

"My dream coaching job is the one I have right now [in Boston]. Obviously, I'd have rather had this job when Larry Bird, Robert Parish, and Kevin McHale were there! I had no intentions of coaching [the 2004-2005 season]. I was going to sit the year out. I told my wife, there are three jobs I'd take if they were open. I told her Boston, New York, or Chicago. When Danny Ainge [the president of the Celtics] came to the house, my wife knew it was over. I was going to take the job! They didn't know it, but I knew it."

Before taking the Celtics job, Rivers was the NBA's Coach of the Year with the Orlando Magic in 1999-2000. In between his time as a bench boss, "Doc" became such an accomplished game analyst that he worked on ABC's number-one team with play-by-play man Al Michaels.

# CHAPTER 5

# Rick Majerus

ick Majerus coached under Al McGuire and Hank Raymonds before becoming the head coach of Marquette himself in 1983. In 1986 Majerus left Marquette to become an assistant for the Milwaukee Bucks under Don Nelson. After one season he returned to head coaching at the collegiate level, leading Ball State and the University of Utah. After leaving Utah he brought his keen knowledge of basketball, candor, and sense of humor to ESPN as a game analyst for the 2004-2005 season. But the itch to coach returned in December 2004 when Majerus was offered—and accepted—the USC coaching job. He was set to get back on the bench for the 2005-2006 season. The Milwaukee native did a sudden about-face when he realized that his health just wasn't up to the level he needed it to be to answer the demands of big-time college coaching. ESPN welcomed Majerus back with open arms.

## Becoming a Member of Al McGuire's Staff

Majerus: "Well, there's a story out there that says Hank Raymonds was hard of hearing, and I was a walk-on and I said, 'I can cover Cobb [a former Marquette player/assistant],' and he thought I said, 'I would like a job!' That story is not true, but—How I got involved in college ball is a great mystery. What happened was,

Rick Majerus gives instructions from the bench.
*From the Marquette University Department of Special Collections and University Archives*

in those days I was a walk-on. In those days they had freshman teams. All they cared about for the last five guys on the freshman team was that they hustled. So I played freshman basketball. I got in a couple games. After that, I hung around. Hank really liked me. He was an instrumental part of that. I really liked listening to him. He was a great teacher. The best professors I had in college were Raymonds and McGuire, although I had some great professors. It started when I got cut in my sophomore year. I went up and coached at Marquette High School. I stayed in touch with Hank and Al. I actually coached McGuire's and Raymonds's sons. Staffs were going from three to four people. Marquette, being Catholic and frugal, they only had two guys. They picked me up. My first contract was for $5,000 for nine months! I wanted three months off in the summer to travel the country and go to basketball camps. There really wasn't any work in the summer, and they didn't have the money to pay me anyway. I think they would have felt guilty paying me $5,000 for 12 months.

"So that's how I got on board.

"When I got there, I remember one day, McGuire said, 'Will you work with the big guys?'

"Hank was working with the guards. That's how I got to work with Jerome Whitehead and those guys. I was fortunate that we had good big guys to work with. Hank was like a co-coach. So I got to go recruiting a lot; that's how I got started."

## Leap Frog

Majerus: "I liked Al's sarcasm, his sense of humor. I remember one year [1974] we were in the Final Four [at Greensboro].

"Al said, 'We're gonna have some fun here today, Rick.'

"Now, he'd never tell that to Hank.

"'Ya see all those coaches up there? They all think that whatever drill we do is gonna be it. Watch, I'm gonna jerk around here. I'm going to tell them that one of the reasons we're such great leapers, and we got quickness is that we do this leap-frog drill in practice.'

"So he has the guys do this stupid leap-frog drill over each other. Sure enough, all these coaches are writing it down, and he'd get asked about it at clinics. Hank was wondering why the hell he was doing it. He thought he was letting them have fun! In his own mind, he was so bored sometimes with the situation, that he just said,

'Well, screw it. I'm going to go out and have some fun here tonight!'"

## The Hickory Hut

Majerus: "It's sad, when I went back to the last Final Four that was held there. The Hickory Hut, which is a place Al took me to, is gone now. A lot of buildings have been torn down, and the arena [The Omni] is gone. I couldn't remember or find the hotel we stayed at. I kind of wanted to go down memory lane. All the physical parts of the memories were gone. It was sad. I remember sitting with Al at The Hickory Hut two nights before we were going to play. He had wanted to get away from everybody. Father Pio, Dr. Eichenberger, they all drove him nuts. I mean that in a nice way. They liked being around him, and they wanted to be a part of it. It was a dive barbecue place. Al would just talk about life, and he'd talk about his kids. I enjoyed those moments the most. He'd talk about players and past players."

## Prayer Fests

Majerus: "One of the great nights I had was with Al, Wayne Embry [former Bucks general manager], and Nellie [former Bucks coach Don Nelson]. They talked about when they played in the NBA and how there were only eight teams and 10 guys on a team. Nowadays, players meet for prayer fests before games, they hug and that. In those days, they said, you hoped even your own teammate got hurt, because that would guarantee another spot on the roster that you would probably have.

"Nellie said, 'I would have had to go back and maybe be a farmer.'

"Al said, 'I would have had to be a cop.'

"I didn't know what I was going to do."

## "I'm That Way Myself!"

Majerus: "Those were always the best nights with McGuire. The game is so different now. He really did love and respect Ray Meyer [the legendary DePaul coach]. Conversely, he hated George Ireland [the former Loyola of Chicago coach]. He thought Ireland was a little bit arrogant. But he said, 'I probably don't like him, because I'm that way myself.' It was fun to see the world according to Al in such intimate detail. Ireland's long dead and Al's dead. I don't think I'm disparaging the dead here. People knew he didn't like Ireland. He was Irish.

"Al would go off on these philosophical tangents and these rants. That was fun for me. Sometimes I'd ask him about certain things. But he didn't really like to talk about the game. After the game was over he'd review it, more so if we lost."

## Recuiting

Majerus: "Al had a feel for recruiting. Once he told me to go visit a kid. Before I did he said, 'Don't worry, that kid's not going to be interested.'

"I said, 'Well then, why am I going out?'

"Al said, 'Because you need to learn that. You need to waste your time and waste money, 'cuz it'll save us time and money in the long run.' He told me, 'Some kid in Nebraska, isn't going to go to Marquette. The way you learn that is by going out there and making that trip.'

"He was right."

## How It Should Be

Majerus: "Al had a philosophy or a belief about the game. There wasn't anything about basketball that you couldn't ask him, that he wouldn't say, 'This is how it should be.' He was very honest about it. In 1976, we lost to Indiana in Alabama [in the NCAA Tournament Mideast Regional]. The two teams were ranked one and two in the country. They had a hell of a team. We did, too. I went in the locker room before that game. He was just shaking. He was so nervous. He had built a monster. The expectations became so great. We had more passionate fans. (We still have those passionate fans.) Al almost felt like the weight of the world was on his shoulders."

## A Fantastic Team

Majerus: "After every trip to Madison, he would marvel at the buildings, the campus, the bell tower, the astronomy department, the medical school, and the labs. Marquette didn't have any of that. When Al came, we had a White Castle on campus. We had a flophouse pool hall. You were involved with the local alcoholics and the street people. It was really what an urban campus was all about at the time, the worst an urban campus is all about. There was no city redevelopment authority. It was remarkable that we did win. McGuire and Raymonds together were a fantastic team. The guys were pretty good guys. They kind of bought into it. You couldn't duplicate it. If you tried to go out and tried to re-create that type of success or that kind of atmosphere, you'd fail. A few guys who tried to coach and be like him failed."

## Not All Basketball

Majerus: "Al gravitated toward Jimmy Taylor at South Alabama and Abe Lemons at Texas. They were guys he loved the most in coaching. They were like him. The guys who took it seriously; he respected that, but he didn't understand it. He didn't understand basketball being so much a part of your life. Those guys couldn't understand his wanting to collect a toy soldier or ride a motorcycle around Lake Michigan. They could see maybe riding a motorcycle. One time Al called Billy Packer [a CBS analyst] and he called me. He said he was going to try to travel on under $100! It was some kind of self-imposed economic sanction!"

## Going out to Dinner

Majerus: "I remember I'd go out with Al and Herb Kohl [the senator from Wisconsin and the Bucks owner] for dinner, and they'd always be pissed because I always grabbed the bill. I owed so much to both of them, and I liked them. Al used to love to stiff guys with the bill. But my whole life I picked it up, because I could never pay him back for everything. He didn't even enjoy that.

"He said, 'I hate going out to dinner with you, because I know you'll buy.'

"He'd lost the competitive game!

"I said, 'Coach, I always feel good about buying, because how do I pay you back?'

"I think he let me do it because he felt it made me feel so good. Al was really a good person, a pretty good guy. He liked to pretend that he didn't know what was going on when he did. He was a complex individual, relatively speaking, yet more predictable than you might have imagined."

## The Deal Maker

Majerus: "What I loved about him the most was [he was] nonjudgmental. A lot of people looked at me as a nerd, or fat, or bald, or whatever. I was the antithesis of a coach. That didn't bother Al. He didn't pigeonhole people. He enjoyed people who were actually more themselves. That's what I think I liked. He didn't try to make me something that I wasn't. When I first got there, if you look at old photos, I have these plaid sport coats. I remember the other assistants talked me into getting them so I could recruit 'the brothers' [African-American athletes]. I'm sittin' there passing like I'm a pimp or something! Al said, 'I used to laugh at that.' But he was kind of a live-and-let-live guy. He was one of those guys who was a deal maker, not a deal breaker. He appreciated self-expression. He was a perfect coach for that era. I think I liked that most about him. Al realized, too, that it was a sport. I tend to be like Lombardi in thinking that I'm plotting the defense of the free world. All coaches are that way, some more than others, but he realized he could have fun. Sometimes, he'd do things to entertain himself!"

## Not the Prototype

Majerus: "He liked the kids' problems. I think the reason he recruited some of those kids is that he liked helping them with those problems. He felt that maybe that was a vehicle to help some guys out. He wouldn't have wanted to coach the prototype North Carolina kid, even if he could. By the prototype Carolina kid, I mean someone who wanted to become a doctor or a lawyer and had a great parent. Yet he and Dean Smith were vanguards, relative to the civil rights movement in basketball. Yet they did it in different ways."

## Motorcycles Versus Traps on Tape

Majerus: "Al really admired Dean Smith for his focus and singleness of purpose, his love of the game.

"Al once said, 'I wish I could be that way.'

"I'd talk with Coach Smith and he'd say, 'I really wish I could take a motorcycle trip.'

"It's like the story of life; sometimes you are who you are, but you wish you could be the other person. The second day on a motorcycle, Dean would want to watch zone traps on tape. After the second day of watching traps on tape, Al would want to be on the motorcycle!"

## Rockaway Beach

Majerus: "He sort of liked to tweak you. He liked to tweak Dean Smith about riding a motorcycle. Dean liked to tweak him. But Al said he wished his son, Allie, had played for Dean Smith for two years and then come to Marquette.

"But Al told me, 'I'll always be thankful that I got to coach him, and we got to be closer.'

"Al was gone a lot. His wife, Pat, raised those kids. He never carried a house key. When I'd drop him off at home, he'd bang on the door. Pat didn't want to leave the door open, although they lived in a very safe neighborhood. He banged on the door at 2 a.m. First of all when she came to the door, he said, 'Who called?' He tried to divert the attention to that.

"He was different in terms of the way he was. He had that remorse about the kids, but he wasn't a guy to stay home and take care of them. He never would buy a shirt or anything like that. One year, he bought a camera. He must have taken 10,000 pictures, if he took one. Then he got rid of the camera. He lost interest in the camera. At the end, even the motorcycle was something where he felt he had to be a 'wild man.' He wanted to do different things. Toward the end of his life I said, 'Why don't we go to New Zealand?' But he never wanted to go back. The only place I ever saw him go back to was Rockaway Beach. He always wanted to do something or see something different. He'd had a good time while he was there, and he felt that time would change that, maybe."

## The Safety Deposit Box

Majerus: "Al had a safety deposit box. I'd go with him once in a while. He had these gold bars. He had these coins from South America. He had a couple diamonds in there. He was always worried that everything was going to crash, and he'd have some kind of commodity! I think his mother was that way."

## Vintage Al

Majerus: "I'll tell you a story. He had a wrapped package for Billy Packer. The three of us were together. I think I was coaching at Ball State. I drove down to meet them at Louisville. He has this wrapped package.

"He called Billy and said, 'Billy, I got a gift for ya.'

"Billy didn't have a gift for him! So Billy went shopping around. He bought Al some shirt at Brooks Brothers. So Al gave Billy the box. He opened it up. It was a weinermobile!

"Billy looked at it and said, 'What's this?'

"Al said, 'It's a weinermobile. It's very valuable.'

"Billy said, 'It is?'

"Al said, 'Yea, I bought them all out. I cornered the market.'

"He wrote on the weinermobile, 'Merry Christmas. Your friend Al.' That weinermobile had about a four-dollar value! Here Billy gave him this shirt!

"Billy said, 'Shit, here I go get him this shirt. I'm under all kinds of pressure, wondering what he got me.'

"Vintage Al!"

## Learning from Al And Hank

Majerus: "Hank [Raymonds] would be more terminology, attention to detail, meticulous preparation. He taught the emphasis on pivoting, pick work, and on the mechanics. Al would be more the psychology of the game and dealing with players, maintaining a calm, having a belief in what you do and not deviating from it. He was great at interacting with players in situations. The coach who's most successful [at the college level] who worked under [Bobby] Knight is 'K' [Mike Krzyzewski] because he deviated the most from Bobby. I'm the only guy really who has been successful who was under Al. When I say successful, I don't mean that egotistically. Very few of the guys who played for him went into coaching. A lot of them tried to be like him. I couldn't be like that. I tried to take the best—him, Hank, and Don Nelson. I made friends with George Karl; I studied the game on my own. I got involved with a great coach by the name of Don Donoher. I recognized that he was a genius. I would always reference McGuire in terms of personnel decisions and psychological things. I always referenced Hank in terms of game plans, practice plans, and film study. That's what Al told me to do. He recognized his shortcomings. Both he and Hank

Rick Majerus talks to a player before a game.
*From the Marquette University Department of Special Collections and University Archives*

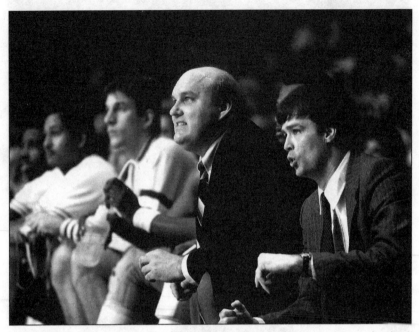

Rick Majerus guided the Warriors to three postseason appearances during his three seasons as head coach.
*From the Marquette University Department of Special Collections and University Archives*

had egos. Hank knew he was an excellent tactician and a great Xs and Os coach. Al realized that he was a great personnel coach/bench coach. He was Phil Jackson before Phil Jackson. Neither of them let that get in the way of each other's success. Hank was very happy. Very few guys would have taken a guy who was one of the leading candidates for the job [at Marquette] and made him his assistant all those years. The interesting thing is they never went to each other's house for dinner. I remained very close to both of them."

## Moving Forward

Majerus: "Joey Meyer [former DePaul head coach] and I talk about this all the time. Of the four coaches at the four prominent schools—Dayton, DePaul, Marquette, and Notre Dame—Digger [Phelps of Notre Dame] had a pretty good career. [Don] Donoher [of Dayton] had a good career. Joey had tough going. You don't want to be a head coach where you grew up as an assistant. I would never hire an assistant coach—very rarely. I would have hired Hank. I shouldn't have gotten hired. That was nice of Hank and Al. I really learned a lot from Nellie. What happened is it was almost too incestuous. I could go to other places. But that year I spent with Nellie [as a Milwaukee Bucks assistant]—he's a great coach—really gave me a different look at things. Plus, I always thought I wanted to coach pro ball. I found out that, for the most part, I didn't.

"I think at Marquette—and I love Hank—I went in and said, 'I'm going to get cars for my assistants.'

"He said, 'Well we never got cars.'

"I said, 'Well, wouldn't you have liked to have a car?'

"He said, 'Yeah.'

"There was always that. I remember when I went to get a weight room.

"Hank said, 'Al didn't have a weight room. He didn't need a weight room.'

"Joey went through that, too. You're better off as an outsider coming in. The best thing that happened to Tom Crean [the current Marquette coach] was when Mike Deane [Crean's predecessor] said Marquette could never get back to the Final Four. That got some guys involved in the program financially. Crean got the [Al McGuire Center]. He had heat in the gym and light in the gym! He got everything that no one else had ever had to that point. When I got into Utah, I got what I wanted. When I look now, the new guy's going to go through some of that, but basically everything's in place. He doesn't need a film room or a weight room. Somebody has to get that going. Donna Shalala [the former University of Wisconsin chancellor] opened up a window for an average student. She opened up the coffers for capital improvements. She got the mindset right. Certainly I think [Pat] Richter [former UW athletic director] is one of the greatest athletic directors in the history of being an AD. But you need someone to move that forward. At Marquette, it got so bogged down under Al. Once The Big East conference came in, we could have taken on Syracuse and Rutgers and those schools on an independent basis. The Big East had the TV contract. Now they had a league affiliation."

## Marquette in The Big East

Majerus: "I don't think Marquette belongs in The Big East now. I think that will be detrimental to them. They can't get into the Big Ten. They don't want to be in Conference USA. They can't make it as an independent. So that's the best option for them.

"Is that going to be good for them? I don't think it's good to be a fringe school, a corner school. Because, let's say they want to recruit a kid in Minnesota, Minnesota doesn't take him, but Iowa will take him. Now that young man's going to play in the Big Ten and get coverage in this area. The only media coverage Marquette is going to get is going to be centered in the East. There's none out there; there's nowhere to move. When we were there, we couldn't get the East schools together. We had played them a couple times a year. We tried to call it a league."

## Basketball Today

Majerus: "I wouldn't change anything in my career. Everyone's tried to live up to McGuire. At Indiana, anybody succeeding Bob Knight has a problem. Look at Mike Davis, I predict he'll be the first Big Ten coach to go. He's removed from Knight's guys. He's a decent coach. But the expectations there are Knight's three national championships. So I think, sometimes, the odds are stacked against you.

"But I loved my time at Marquette. There isn't anything I wouldn't do for them. I've got great friends. The priests were tremendous. I met some of the finest human beings. The professors were great teachers. So much of what I believe, I would attribute to those people at Marquette. I really think I tried to do the best I could to get away from Hank and Al in terms of finding out more about the game. But it's hard to do that in a week in the summer or a three-day weekend. That experience with Don Nelson was great. I don't know if Hank was ever appreciated for what a great job he did under very difficult circumstances. His first year, we got upset by Miami University in Ohio [in the NCAA Tournament]. People don't realize to this day what a great team Miami had. They think it was a shortcoming of the Marquette team. Just like at Kentucky. Marquette was never given credit for beating that Kentucky team coached by Adolf Rupp. The disparaging remarks are directed at Rupp. Marquette isn't given credit for a great game that year. That's just the way it is; that's just the way sports are. Between Deane, Dukiet, Crean, McGuire, Raymonds, and myself, there are so many diverse personalities that have come out of the Marquette program. A lot of it, too, is your president. Father [Albert] DiUlio [MU president from 1990-1996] was all for athletics. Father [John] Raynor [MU president from 1965-1990] was sort of, but not as committed as Father [Robert] Wild [MU president from 1996-present] is currently. I think Al was underappreciated. That statement, 'A prophet in his own land is never appreciated.' I think that was the case with Al those last four or five years of his career. Just like history will treat Bill Clinton better later than now. As Al said, 'I couldn't have made it today.' If he had slapped Bernard Toone in the face, in this day and age with all the media outlets, I mean, geez, he'd have been on Rush Limbaugh, and then Al Sharpton would be coming in. I had a player at Utah in the Final Four in 1998, where the Carolina kid, Makhtar Ndiaye, said [the Utah player] called him a nigger. Ndiaye has since apologized. He said it wasn't true. We had just beaten Carolina. We were having a phenomenal year. All of a sudden, the whole focus going into the national championship game was mitigating the damage of this Carolina kid blaming a Mormon kid. The media is so pervasive nowadays. Al and Knight and those guys didn't have to deal with that back then. They could control it. Now a days, it's so mean-spirited. I sensed that even last year [2003-2004] with Marquette.

MU's only the second school in history to not make the NCAA Tournament, one year after going to the Final Four. Now there's this undercurrent out there about Crean."

## The Final Four

Majerus: "When we went to the Final Four [with Marquette in 1977], sneaking someone in the back door was not that difficult! When I went with Utah, there were media obligations. And 64 teams—remember there were only 32 teams when Marquette went in 1977. There wasn't as much parity. A lot of it is injury and the right guys. A lot of it with the Final Four is that's what Tom Crean will be held to. At Utah, we made the Final Four, and we went to the tournament every year after that. We only lost in the first round once. But people always said, 'Are they going to get back there?' Tom will be haunted by that. It's going to be difficult for him. I think he realizes that."

# CHAPTER 6

# Bob Dukiet

**"H**e was a good coach." Those were the words of Hank Raymonds in describing Bob Dukiet, "The Piano Man." He earned that nickname from the Milwaukee media, because of his talent with the keys. Unfortunately, the charming Easterner couldn't play a sweet enough tune as a coach at MU. The former assistant at Princeton University appeared to be a star in the making. Dukiet, who'd been a standout player at Boston College, was handsome, charming, and well liked. Those qualities helped him become a good recruiter. After leaving the Tigers, Bob went on to St. Peter's College, a low Division I school, as head coach. He put the New Jersey school on the map, in the mid-1980s, getting them to the NCAA Tournament on numerous occasions, while winning 70 percent of his games.

At Marquette, Dukiet had a respectable 1986-1987 season, which included a 16-13 record, and a first-round loss at Nebraska in the National Invitation Tournament. But a 10-18 record the following season was followed by a 13-15 mark in 1988-1989. Bob Dukiet was fired in the spring of 1989.

*Author's note: Dukiet politely declined to be interviewed for this book. Evidently, the memories of his time in Southeastern Wisconsin are too painful.*

Bob Dukiet "The Piano Man" had difficulty finding the right "note" during his tenure.
*From the Marquette University Department of Special Collections and University Archives*

## Hank Raymonds on Dukiet

Raymonds: "I was the athletic director then. Now, you have to understand at Marquette, not one person at that time made any kind of decision to hire anybody. We had I don't know how many committees, how many interviews there were of different people. When it got down to it, the consensus then was to go with Bob Dukiet [to replace Rick Majerus, who'd moved on to be an assistant for the Bucks]. One of the reasons was that Hubie Brown [a former NBA coach and NBA TV analyst] who was respected by the media, as well as in sports circles, along with Jud Heathcoate [a former Michigan State coach] were people who highly recommended Bob for the job. Hubie, I guess, was pretty close to him, because Hubie had watched him and observed him; he was doing a good job at St. Peter's. Then he came to Marquette; unfortunately, he had some problems. Basketball-wise, he wasn't a bad coach.

"He had a great personality with his music and everything. After that, that was about it. I guess it was a little different with the media than coming from the East where he was. He did well prior to that. He always did; he was always a good coach. Ric Cobb [former MU star and assistant coach under Rick Majerus] was going to stay as an assistant with Bob, and then something happened. Ric had been a candidate for the job, along with about five or six people. Bob was going to keep Ric; then something happened between them—I don't know what it was—and then that was the end. It didn't work out.

"It's hard to say [why he wasn't successful]; everyone's different in how they act. But I personally liked Bob. It's just hard to explain. I just think some people wanted him out of there. They didn't exactly not win; they were winning, but not the way they wanted him to.

"Bob went on to have pretty good teams at Gannon University. It wasn't poor coaching. I guess maybe there wasn't the talent level. At Marquette we were spoiled all the time."

## Clyde Rusk on Dukiet

Venerable Clyde Rusk was a successful, longtime high school coach in Wisconsin. He met up with Dukiet when the latter was recruiting one of his players, Trevor Powell, who eventually came to Marquette.

Rusk: "Dukiet was a very enthusiastic and very intelligent person. Of course, he had the musical background; he played the piano. He was a good conversationalist; he was willing to communicate in a lot of different areas. He did a very good job [recruiting Powell]. Trevor wanted to stay in the Milwaukee area. He was recruited very normally and up front. Trevor went there. Bob asked me to give critiques of the [Marquette] games, and afterward, he asked if I might help him; and I did that. The following year, he asked me if I wanted to be a volunteer assistant. I thought it would be a good way to view Division I from a lot of different areas. I went with him the third [and last] year.

"The basketball that he learned he taught extremely well. He had a special way of teaching that zone defense that he had. That was effective against teams of similar talent to ours. I think we needed more talent. Tony Smith [a former Milwaukee area star who went on to an NBA career] came on strong his junior year. We moved him to point guard. That really helped him a lot. We were competitive for the most part. But a lot of games we couldn't win. Oregon State [with eventual NBA star Gary Payton] beat us by just three. We were awfully close to having a winning season that last year.

"Toward the end, the media actually came down to see who was late for practice. They were just looking for things, anything that was negative. That was just a [hard] thing to stay positive, and the kids fought through that pretty well. I think a factor was that he didn't get a couple more players. I think if we'd had just one really outstanding player at that time, we would have been in the win column, anyway. He was very personable. He got along with some of the kids very well. Tony Smith got along with him very well. At

Trevor Powell scored 1,571 points and pulled in 765 rebounds during his four years in Blue and Gold. *From the Marquette University Department of Special Collections and University Archives*

Bob Dukiet now leads a laidback life as a professional piano player.
*From the Marquette University Department of Special Collections and University Archives*

that time, I don't think anybody knew how good Tony was going to be. That move [Dukiet] made to move Smith to point guard was a big factor. The next year he did very well for [coach] Kevin [O'Neill]. They gave a lot of credit to Kevin for Tony being a point guard when actually he'd started the previous year."

## Dukiet After Marquette

Dukiet rebounded nicely with a successful stint at Gannon University in Pennsylvania. He led that program to the Elite Eight of the NCAA Division II Tourney. After eight seasons, he left in 1996.

What is "The Piano Man" up to these days? During Marquette's run to the Final Four under Tom Crean, Phil Mushnick of the *New York Post* caught up with the 55-year-old lifelong bachelor.

Dukiet, who resides in Boynton Beach, Florida, plays the piano for a living.

He told Mushnick, "I'll run the gamut, from formal affairs at country clubs, the Marriott in Delray Beach, to senior citizen gatherings. These days, I'm 'Piano Bob' of Palm Beach County. I'll play for anyone whose feet still move. I work up a sweat and they like me."

# Tony Smith

Tony Smith was one of the few bright spots for Marquette during Bob Dukiet's tenure. The guard from Wauwautosa earned an Associated Press All-America honorable mention as he led the Warriors into an appearance in the NIT. Smith finished his Marquette career with 1,688 points, currently ranking him as Marquette's fifth all-time leading scorer. Drafted in the second round of the NBA draft in 1990 by the Los Angeles Lakers, Smith played in the NBA for nine seasons for six different teams (Los Angeles Lakers, Miami Heat, Phoenix Suns, Charlotte Hornets, Milwaukee Bucks, and Atlanta Hawks).

## MU Career

Smith: "Well, I think coming out of high school, I wasn't really a blue-chipper, somebody everyone was after around the country. I think I made up my mind pretty early that I was basically going to stay in state. I was looking at Marquette, Wisconsin, and UW-Green Bay because [coach Dick] Bennett was there. I wound up choosing Marquette. I liked the fact that it was fairly close. At that point, I was being recruited by [assistant] Ric Cobb and [head coach] Rick Majerus. Those guys were coaching at that point. When I actually got to Marquette, those guys were gone. Bob Dukiet had come in.

Tony Smith holds Marquette's all-time single-season scoring average lead with a 23.8 point-per-game average during the 1989-1990 season.

*From the Marquette University Department of Special Collections and University Archives*

That was a bit of a shock, because those guys were just part of the reason I had picked Marquette. I really liked that fact that it was close to home. I like to think of myself as someone who adapts to whatever. At that point, I was thinking that I had confidence in myself as a player. There wasn't really much I could do about that. I was just going to go where I wanted to go, and to whomever they brought in to coach I was just going to have to prove that I was recruited for a good reason and I belonged there. That was my mindset when the coaching changes came about."

## Move to Point Guard

Smith: "It was a change, but I didn't really go to the point until my junior year. It was just another thing that I had to adapt to. The team needed me at that position. It took me a while to learn before I felt natural with what the point guard was supposed to do. I played in high school [at Wauwautosa East near Milwaukee] with a best friend who was the point guard so I didn't have to play that position. I just ran around at shooting guard and did whatever."

## MU Needed More Talent

Smith: "I think we were more than one player short; I think we were a couple. It depends on the caliber of player. I think of some of those players who had transferred in [when Kevin O'Neill became coach] and we practiced with my senior year—like Keith Stewart and Ron Curry—I think if we'd have had those guys my senior year, we would have had a good year. I'm almost positive we would have been in the NCAA Tournament."

MU went to the NIT in Smith's senior season.

"We lost to some good teams that year: Virginia, Michigan had a great team that year. We played some good teams, played 'em close. We won some. Obviously, we didn't win enough to get to the NCAA; I think with those guys we would have."

## Dukiet/O'Neill Personalities

Smith: "I'm not rattled by the personalities of certain people. Maybe someone who's quirky—take O'Neill, for example. He'd go off on you at the drop of a dime. My whole thing—and this is the way I operated in my NBA career with several coaches—was to respect the position of coaching, no matter who it was. A coach is there to teach, to motivate, and to try to get the best out of his guys. Now, he might have the wrong impression of how to do that. When you're coaching, you're dealing with a lot of different personalities. There are some guys you can yell at, and other guys you can't yell at. It's up to him to try to find that fine line, where he gets the best out of each guy. If someone yells at me, I just take it that he's trying to help me. As a player, you know if you screw up or not. You expect to get yelled at. It's no surprise; it's not something that you should take personally. If I screw up, I deserve to get yelled at. Big deal. This guy, maybe he yells more than normal. But who cares? It doesn't matter. You just go out there and try not to make the same mistake again.

"I think Dukiet was a big screamer, but he wasn't like Kevin. Dukiet was kind of a weird guy. You didn't know what was going to happen during the practice. One day he came in, and he wasn't talking. Something had happened in the media. He had this towel on his head; he was playin' a sheik. It was the funniest thing I ever saw; he didn't speak the whole practice.

"I don't remember Dukiet's last days as coach. I wasn't into all that. My only thing about the Dukiet era was I was a little disappointed about the recruiting during those years. We weren't getting any players who were at the level that they should be here at Marquette. That hurt us. My freshman year when we came, we had a decent squad with [David] Boone, [Mike 'Pops'] Sims, and those guys. The next couple years, we didn't bring in anybody of that caliber. We didn't improve as a team during those years. That's the only thing that I regretted, because when you're in college, you at least want to make the NCAA Tourney once.

"The thing I remember most about K.O. [Kevin O'Neill] was when he first got the job. The first time we even met him, he came in on a tirade. He didn't come in and say hello; he didn't say anything! His first words were going off on people. It was because our grades were so bad. He was upset about the grades that we had. He didn't even say hello. He just started in. He was screamin' and yellin', but like I said before, inside of my head, I was just laughing!"

## MU Memories

Smith: "I have a lot of good memories of being at Marquette—from the guys in my dorm my freshman year. It's funny; I don't remember a lot of road trips, that type of stuff. I remember a few games here and there that stick out in my mind.

"I wish I had had maybe a couple more years with Kevin, and the guys he was bringing in. He could recruit; I thought the guys that practiced with us my senior year, they were the caliber of player that I was expecting when I came in to Marquette. But, as I look back, I say, 'Okay, if we'd have done that recruiting, there's a chance that I would never have been at the point guard position. So, it's a double-edged sword. I'm going to stick with the way it turned out.'"

## Ever Dream You'd Play in the NBA?

Smith: "I'm sure I wasn't thinking that way, coming out of Marquette. I can't remember being in the school thinking, 'Well, I'm going to be in the pros next year.' It wasn't like that back then. Now, guys are thinking that in high school. Back then, I wasn't really that concerned with it. Our team wasn't doing that well. I didn't think that I'd get much attention. I didn't know what was going on. After the season was over, you started going to camps and playing with all the other guys who were supposedly the tops in the nation. You see you can play with 'em. Then, thoughts start creeping into your head. I did the same thing in high school. I was at one of the Nike All-Star camps. You had all the guys there, and you're playin' with 'em."

Tony Smith tries to keep his balance along the sideline.
*From the Marquette University Department of Special Collections and University Archives*

## Tony Smith's Post-NBA Career

Smith: "I was scouting for the Milwaukee Bucks, trying to get back into basketball. I had gotten married before that and moved out to L.A. That was part of the reason I quit playing. I had thought about starting a family. I went through a divorce and wanted to get back in. The scouting didn't work out; I may have needed more experience. So I think about basketball; I'm contemplating working with young kids, doing camps here and there. You have so much knowledge; you just want to pass it on. I'll try the coaching; I don't know if I'll even like it. Scouting wasn't bad. But it's nothing long term. I didn't feel any real involvement. You were kinda off on your own, just going to random games, watching players, and evaluating them. Your interaction with the actual team is very limited. I wanted to be more in there with a team and have some kind of input. I think assistant coaching would be a better fit for that.

"I'm going back to Marquette for my degree. I was in engineering, but to do that, I'd have to get back into the math first. It would probably be more work than if I started something new. Marquette has some stuff worked out for me. I think I'm going to go the route of leadership and organization and I can transfer some of my old credits."

# CHAPTER 8

# Kevin O'Neill

K evin O'Neill came to Marquette before the 1989-1990 season. Previously, O'Neill had served as an assistant at the University of Arizona from 1986 to 1989. When he was at Arizona, O'Neill once showed up wearing a gorilla outfit for a recruit! K.O. could recruit. He loved the challenge of rebuilding programs, and he got the chance to do that at Marquette. He inherited a Warriors team that was trying to regain its identity as a top college basketball team. His team became a member of the Midwestern Collegiate Conference (now Horizon League) his first year. Marquette had been an independent up to that point. The Warriors also landed back in postseason tournament play as Marquette went to the NIT in O'Neill's first year. After two years in the Midwestern Collegiate Conference, O'Neill's Warriors pioneered a new conference, the Great Midwest Conference. The fledgling conference was a step up in competition as Cincinnati, DePaul, and Memphis joined Marquette. O'Neill earned Great Midwest Conference Coach of the Year honors in 1993 and 1994, with his 1994 team earning the conference regular-season championship with a 10-2 conference record and a bid to the NCAA Tournament where the Warriors upset Kentucky in the second round.

Kevin O'Neill returned Marquette to a level of prominence during his years as head coach. *From the Marquette University Department of Special Collections and University Archives*

After compiling an 86-62 record over five years, including going 44-17 over his final two years, O'Neill left Marquette to become the head coach at the University of Tennessee. He is now an assistant coach with the Indiana Pacers.

## Early Years

O'Neill: "There were many days in those first three years when I didn't know if we'd make it or not. There were a lot of long days. At the same time, there were really a lot of rewards. To watch that freshman class of [Damon] Key, [Robb] Logterman, and [Jim] McIlvaine actually put this place on the map themselves. They went from being booed as freshmen to being cheered as seniors. That was a real thrill for me."

## Tough Love

O'Neill: "I think it's our jobs as coaches to give young people a chance to make it. The only way they get that chance is if you find out a little bit about them as people, as well as players, and treat them as such. They're people, too, who have goals and have insecurities even at the highest level. It's our job to help them along the way."

## Never Get Caught Unprepared

O'Neill: "There were so many things that happened while I was here. That was my first coaching job at the major college level. I was laughing about that with [Michigan State coach] Tom Izzo. We were talking about never getting surprised in coaching. I will never forget it. I was playing Notre Dame here my first year.

"We hadn't beaten them in a while. We were up big, 10 or 11 points in the final three or four minutes. They went into a 1-3-1 zone. I'll never forget sitting there as a coach going, 'Oh ****, we didn't cover that!' We almost lost the game! From that point on, I said, 'I will never get caught unprepared again.' There were many things here at Marquette. Milwaukee's still a place that has fond memories for me."

## The Sweet 16 Season

O'Neill: "I thought we had a chance to be pretty good. I thought we had a better team than people thought.

"Those guys had really paid their dues. That group of seniors, Robb and Mac and Damon had endured some booing as freshmen; they'd endured a lot of things. They had grown up and played together for a while. We had some depth. We had a great point guard in Tony Miller. I thought we had a chance to be good, but you never know how it's going to shake out. But I thought our guys really made a good run, and played hard and well together.

"They became a group that was really resilient. All of them, in my estimation, were under-recruited, so they had a chip on their shoulder from day one. Like all young guys, they probably thought, as freshmen and sophomores, that it was going to be easier than it was. But when it came right down to it, they really toughened up and hardened up as a group. They learned that it only matters what is done within the team. They became oblivious to everything other than trying to win and practice hard and do the right thing. That's a group you can never forget when you're coaching them for a four-year period."

## Beating Kentucky with Lute's Help

O'Neill: "I did talk to [Arizona coach] Lute [Olson] as soon as we knew what our matchup was after the first-round game. [When I was at Arizona], we had always had great success in attacking presses in tournaments; that led to layups and good shots. His whole thing was: 'They're going to have a big guy in the front of the press. You want Tony [Miller] to be a guy who just goes right at that big guy.' That's what we tried to do the entire time was line up that big guy with the ball and have our point guard go right at him and away from the point guard. When we did, we ended up with a lot of four-on-three and five-on-four opportunities. We got some early three-point shots out of Robb, and easy shots—some layups and easy baskets. We really got off to a good start and held 'em off down the stretch.

"We wanted to get out to a great start, which we were able to do. The whole time we were building the lead, I knew that great teams who have great coaches, like Rick Pitino, are going to come back and make a run at you. We all understood that. We said it at halftime; we said it going down the stretch. We just said we weren't interested in anything but winning this game. We did a good job off holding them off down the stetch. I believe they cut it to one or two points a couple different times.

"Our guys responded with big baskets and big plays on defense, and had great rebounding efforts down the stretch on the defensive board. We were able to come away with a win and gave ourselves a chance to play Duke in the Sweet 16.

"I felt like we had arrived where, in my mind, we were one of the country's premier programs. But honestly, the first thought I had was 'Who were we going to play next?' At the time we really didn't know, but my thoughts were racing ahead. I really thought that team could win the national championship. I may have been the only one that believed it, but I thought once we got by Kentucky, we had as good a chance as anybody. It was very gratifying; it was a big win; it meant a lot to the Marquette fans, to me personally, and to the people around me, but at the same time, I guess I was doing the old coach thing where I was trying to get the next win."

## Duke in the Sweet 16

O'Neill: "We did give a great effort. It was heartbreaking that we couldn't finish the job and get to the Final Four and have a chance to play for the national title. But once the game was done, I had a chance to go in and tell the guys how much I appreciated their effort. It was a great year that year. It was a great five years that I had in Milwaukee.

"I left there feeling like we had done the job we were supposed to do."

## Left Too Soon?

O'Neill: "If I had to do it again, would I have stuck around a little longer? In retrospect, probably. The grass always looks greener on the other side. But once I left and went other places, I found out what a great place [Marquette] was, and what a great city this was.

"I was young and foolish. But I don't have any regrets. I haven't had any regrets in my whole life, to be honest with you. But I feel blessed and fortunate I can just coach in this great game and be a part of it because it's a wonderful way to make a living and be around people."

## Building up Marquette

O'Neill: "Of all the things I've done in coaching—and I've been fortunate enough to coach in the playoffs, be a head coach in the NBA, go to Final Fours; I've been blessed with a great deal of accomplishments throughout my career—I can honestly say it was very gratifying to take a program from where it was to where we ended up. The thing that people forget is that we decided to join the Great Midwest [Conference], and we were in the MCC [Midwestern Collegiate Conference]. That to me was a huge challenge for our program. It was the best thing we had done. It was the best thing we had done at Marquette University in a long time. Taking on that challenge in that league at that time was the right thing to do. But it made the job all the harder at that time, yet all the more gratifying when it was done.

"I've coached a lot of places since, and have now been on the pro level for a while. A lot of people still remember me as the guy who coached at Marquette. That was my first major college head coaching job. It was a great time in my life; I really enjoyed it. I appreciated the confidence [MU athletic director] Bill Cords and the Marquette community showed in me.

Kevin O'Neill diagramed a winning strategy against Kentucky in the 1994 NCAA Tournament. He told guard Tony Miller to keep dribbling against the press and take it right at the Kentucky big man.

*From the Marquette University Department of Special Collections and University Archives*

"I still have a soft spot for Milwaukee and Marquette; because I loved living there; I loved coaching at that school.  It was a great time in my life, and a great experience."

# CHAPTER 9

# Jim McIlvaine

W hen Jim "Big Mac" McIlvaine was at MU, he was often viewed as too gangly, too awkward to go to the next level. But Kevin O'Neill, his coach at the time, predicted that McIlvaine would become a millionaire because of basketball. "K.O." turned out to be a prophet when McIlvaine signed a multimillion-dollar free agent contract with Seattle after being drafted in the second round by the Washington Bullets in 1994.

## Coming to Marquette/The Kevin O'Neill Era

McIlvaine: "It seemed like a weird era when I was there; it was like a transitional thing. When I showed up, there were a bunch of guys there that Kevin [O'Neill] didn't recruit, but at the same time, he was willing to honor their scholarships. But you could tell he wanted to get those guys out of there and get in his own guys as quick as he could.

"We helped turn the corner, and it all goes back to Kevin, because it was his vision and his drive and determination to get the right guys in. He wanted to get the right people into the program and infuse energy into it. There seemed to be a mentality, even while I was there that, 'We won the championship in 1977, why can't you do that again?' It seemed that people couldn't grasp how hard it was

Jim McIlvaine goes up for a rebound.

*From the Marquette University Department of Special Collections and University Archives*

to get to that level and be there and stay there. How much money it took to really get a program to be at that level. How important so many things were, like the recruiting process, to convince kids to show up there. Coming from a program like Arizona, Kevin knew what it took to get to the Final Four and be one of the top contenders every year, not only in terms of winning games, but in terms of getting the best recruits from all over the country. It goes back to him.

"Kevin put the right pieces in the puzzle and made [Marquette] an attractive job again. When he came in, it wasn't a job that a lot of coaches looked at and said, 'Hey, if I could get that Marquette job.'

"Part of it was the conference we were in. First, not being in a conference and being an independent. Then, the transition and finding the right conference. You have to find the right level of basketball that we needed to be at to convince guys that this is the program you want to play for because you're going to face top teams. Maybe some guys want to go to a conference where they know they're going to win the conference championship every year. But for a lot of guys, you want to play against Cincinnati and Louisville and Kentucky. Kevin certainly had the experience and the background to know what it took to take the program back to that mode."

## Free Tickets

McIlvaine: "Coach Dukiet [O'Neill's predecessor] was a nice guy. I talked to him several times, but Marquette wasn't a program I was seriously looking at when he was still there. They gave me complimentary tickets to the games when I was in high school. Everything was cool with the NCAA. I could take the tickets and go watch the games. I'd do it because I had friends in high school who wanted to go to the games. They just thought it was the greatest. 'How did you get these tickets?' they'd ask. So we'd go, but I wanted to go somewhere warm. Nobody had really made the compelling argument for me to stick around the basketball programs in Wisconsin. There wasn't that much that was desirable about them. Tony Smith had helped turn Marquette around a little bit, but he was just one guy. It was like how often are you going to get a guy like Tony Smith in when the program was at that level?"

## Choosing MU Over Wisconsin

McIlvaine: "I didn't know Robb [Logterman] that well. We played in [former UW coach] Steve Yoder's basketball camp together in fifth or sixth grade. For anybody who doesn't think a school's college basketball camp is important for the program, that week alone sealed it for me that I didn't need to go to Wisconsin because I saw Yoder at the beginning of the week, and then I saw him again at the end of the week. He showed up to give his son some trophy. I stayed at the dorms in Wisconsin. It wasn't a pleasant experience.

"I knew Robb from that experience. He could really shoot the basketball. I got to know Damon [Key]. We played against each other in high school. I played on [former Marquette player/assistant coach] Ric Cobb's AAU team. It just felt so good to have Damon as my power forward. He was such a good scorer. We complemented each other well. It seemed like such a natural fit [to continue the run at Marquette]. Our AAU team made it to the finals at Vegas. We beat so many good teams. I loved playing with those guys [at Marquette]."

## Straight Shooter

McIlvaine: "[Kevin O'Neill] was a smooth salesman. It wasn't so much that he always told you what you wanted to hear, but he knew when he had to tell you stuff that you had to hear. He had that genius about him that you didn't always necessarily get from other coaches.

"After I got out of school, I was trying to hire an agent.

"Kevin said, 'Ask everybody who you're considering for an agent to tell you who they would tell their son to choose as an agent if they couldn't represent him. You'll see how truthful they'll be, and how much they'll look after you by the answers they give you.'

"I asked the other agents; they always gave me the safe answers like, 'Oh there's this guy who used to represent basketball players, but I think he's retired now.' Or, 'There's a guy who's really good, but I think he only represents football players.' The guy I ended up hiring told me straight out, he said, 'Hire Bill Strickland, he's the most honest, trustworthy guy out there of the whole group.' Kevin seemed like the kind of guy, that, if you asked him point blank, 'I'm not going to go to Marquette. What do you think the best school to go to would be?' He'd tell ya. He wouldn't pull any punches or tell you to go to a school outside the conference, so he wouldn't have to face you. He might have told me to go to Wisconsin and stay in state. This program's going to turn around. They're not going to keep Steve Yoder there forever. They are going to get in some fresh blood! He probably would have given me that honest answer. He was funny, when he needed to be, and entertaining, but he gave you the straight answers."

## O'Neill's Aspirations

McIlvaine: "Once I got out of Marquette, I was still in contact with Kevin on a regular basis at Tennessee and then at Northwestern. He made it clear that his No. 1 goal was to be an NBA assistant.

"He said, 'That's the job for me. You don't have to worry about any of this recruiting stuff. You don't have to deal with 17-year-old kids dictating what happens to your career.'

"At the time, it seemed like he really wanted to be a NBA assistant. He got the NBA assistant jobs. In the back of my mind, I think he wanted to be a head coach just to say that he was a head coach and has coaching experience in the NBA for when Lute Olson retires at Arizona.

"I think he'd be a guy who'd really like to go back there. He may not think it, or admit it, or own up to it at this point. The whole time I was at Marquette he'd always talk about how great things were at Arizona and how Lute had the world by the tail. When we went back out there and played, it was like a welcome home party for Kevin. He was the guy who recruited Sean Elliott, Brian Williams, Steve Kerr, and that whole crew. He was the one everybody out there gave credit to for bringing those guys in. It's the one place in the basketball world that Kevin hasn't burned any bridges."

## Studies/Playing Ball

McIlvaine: "I found a smart girlfriend who would help me study because I was in the school of business for two and a half years. That was a mistake. I was never going to get out of there in four years if I stayed in business. That's why I ended up going over to communications. I'd sit through a class like statistics. One of the cool things about going to Marquette was that I had 30 kids from my high school going there. There were always familiar faces around. One of the kids in my class was John DeRose. Statistics was like nothing for him. He didn't study for it, but he still got As on his tests. I studied my brains out and got 62. That was what turned the tide for me. During my last class we had a Pass/Fail, where if you failed the class it didn't count against your GPA. To stay out of mandatory study hall you had to have a 2.5 GPA. I barely passed statistics. It was borderline. I had to go back to the teacher and ask her not to fail me. Otherwise, I would have been back into study hall! Once I got into communications, it was smooth sailing."

## Hard Practices

McIlvaine: "There were easy practices. As the season wore on, Kevin knew he couldn't push us as hard as he did earlier in the season. But there were hard practices. For me the running always got me. It wasn't so much the running itself; it was the time.

"There were some practices where we'd screw up and do a lot of running. It wasn't like the whole team screwed up; one guy would screw up and everybody had to run. You had to do deep sixes the length of the court six times in 32 or 33 seconds. The managers would keep track of the game clock, so you would know. They were always over there turning it on and turning it off to make sure everybody could get it in time. Because after an hour and a half of practicing, if he puts you on the line and makes you do a bunch of deep sixes, there's no way even the fastest guys would be able to do it. Tony Miller would still be able to do it. Tony Smith would still be able to do it, but the rest of us were dragging. There's no way Damon [Key] and I could do it. Damon's mouth looked like he'd just gotten done eating a powdered donut. I'd be over in the corner puking in a garbage can. There's no way I could have run a deep six in 32, but the managers were over there turning the clock on and off, so we'd get time.

"Kevin knew it, but we didn't know that he knew it. Every once in a while, if he got really frustrated with us, he'd say, 'Shut the clock off, give me the stopwatch.'

"You could run that thing in 20 seconds, he'd say, 'Thirty-four! Go to the other end!' It didn't matter what was on the stopwatch. His goal and intention was to put you on the line and make you run."

## O'Neill and Logterman's Relationship

McIlvaine: "Dysfunctional, bizarre. Things were different at the NBA level, but I've never seen a player/coach relationship like they had. They were very, very close with each other. In the group, in front of the team, Robb was Coach's whipping boy. But when they were alone, Kevin was much cooler with Robb and got along a lot better with him.

"It never got to the point where Robb was going to transfer or considered transferring. Well, we all did at some point, but never serious discussions where he just couldn't handle it and wanted to get out. The natural progression of things was that as Robb got older he didn't make as many mistakes, especially when he went back to his natural two [guard] position. Some of the focus got shifted off

Robb and on to somebody else like Shannon Smith or other guys, and they just couldn't take the heat and had to get out of the kitchen. It didn't matter how many times [assistant coach] Craig McMillan came over, he'd say, 'Don't worry; let the swear words go in one ear and out the other, just listen to the message in between.' Some guys just didn't know it was going to be that taxing. I just had to repeat the mantra in my own head that [assistant coach] Dan Theiss gave me. He'd say, 'Remember, if you can get through four years of Kevin O'Neill, you can get through anything!'

"Every year, we'd do our preseason conditioning; it was like miniature celebrations. Junior year it was, 'We've only got one more first day of conditioning.' The next year we had all these milestones about that stuff. At least I know I did in my head. I'd say, 'Robb, guess what? If we had eight conditioning sessions this year, and eight next year, that means we're under a dozen for our career here. We're almost done!' And then you'd go over to the freshman and say, 'Man, you've got two dozen more conditioning sessions you're going have to do.' We'd rub it in a little bit."

## O'Neill, Tough and Caring

McIlvaine: "As a player, sometimes you're not sure that a coach cares. You're smart enough at that age to say, 'What's his real motivation? Does he really want to see me do better, or is he just trying to save his job, or get to the next spot?' I think by the time Kevin got down to Knoxville and we all had a good idea that he was going to coach Tennessee, we said, 'Why aren't you swearing at us, Coach?' He cared, so did we.

"From a basketball perspective, they always seemed to have a purpose in mind. His demands weren't unrealistic. I was actually kind of surprised. One of the things Kevin had us do was a mile run in preseason. It was 6 a.m. on a Saturday. Everybody had a time that they had to make. That was another Robb abuse thing. Since he was in cross-country, he was expected to go faster than everybody else. He had to do a time of 4:52 or something like that. In my freshman year, I had to do 6:30. I was struggling to do that. You had four weekends to make your time. If you didn't make your time, you had to go out to the track after practice and try to make your time. Jay Zulauf [a former MU player] might have been the only guy who had to go out and do that. By the last weekend, I was trying to make my time. Rod Gross was pushing me in the back. Mark Anglavar's pulling me by my shirt. Robb's pushing me, 'All right, just move your legs. Keep it straight. Don't fall.' I did better as a sophomore and junior. But by my senior year, my time went back up to 6:30. I couldn't figure out why, but I wasn't about to question it. I kept working. I ended up running it at 5:50, with nobody's help, either. I think the coaches played with the clock. It was one less night of the week that you'd go out and party!"

## K.O.'s Temper

McIlvaine: "We lost a game, I think it was St. Louis, that we shouldn't have lost. K.O. was irate. After we get back to our rooms, Robb and I sat there. We'd try to analyze it. We'd say, 'Do you think he was really angry and threw the glass at the door, because he knew we were all sitting there in the hallway and we'd all jump about four feet when it smacked against the door? Was he really that angry, or did he do that for dramatic effect?' Sometimes, he'd do that to scare a guy. That's a good reason that they only have four years of college eligibility. After that, you figure the coach out. That stuff doesn't work anymore. Once on the road, Kevin got so mad at somebody that he punched a locker. I think he broke his hand. It was swollen up. He didn't want to give anybody the satisfaction of knowing he was hurt. So he wouldn't do anything about it.

"I don't think there's a Division I school closer to my house, 20 some minutes door to door, but I never spent another night in my own bed, once I came up [to Marquette]. I was a little nervous; that was kind of a psychological thing Kevin would do. He didn't really push me that hard. He knew it would work by pushing Robb, and Robb and I being in the same apartment. I see that. I didn't want any of that wrath coming down on me. I wasn't going to get out of line anyway.

"I'd say, 'I could stay overnight at my house, but I have practice tomorrow at 11.'

"I had to be there. I met my wife at the end of my freshman year. We'd go back to her house in Janesville. If I had practice the next day at 11, she'd say, 'Well we could stay overnight and leave early in the morning.' I'd say, 'Yeah, but I could have a flat tire, or, weather could change. Let's just go back tonight, and then I'll have a good night's sleep. I won't sleep for anything, if I'm 90 miles away from practice, and I've only got five hours to get there!' It was one of those things where if you're not working, somebody else is working. He might get it because he did that little extra."

## Staying in Shape

O'Neill's insistence on being a taskmaster helped Big Mac make a bundle of money in the NBA.

McIlvaine: "I got married right out of school. The day after the wedding, I flew out to go to the summer league games. We waited six weeks to go on our honeymoon. Even then, I brought a jump rope with me. I ran around on the island trying to stay in shape. I would get so paranoid and so nervous about showing up to the first day of practice not being in good enough shape."

## Parents—Keep Your Mouth Shut!

McIlvaine: "I don't have any coaching aspirations, not beyond fourth or fifth grade. Beyond that, the parents get way too serious. I think what drove it home for me was Jeff Zavada's parents and Jay Zulauf's parents. I don't want to say anything that would be taken in the wrong way, but it wasn't what they said to their kids; it was what they said to Kevin. Don't you know how much you're screwing this up for your son by bothering the coach? My parents, thank goodness, didn't have any ability to play sports. They were happy to say, 'Hey Coach, how ya doin?' We'd lose by 15 points to a team we weren't supposed to lose to, and my dad would be there saying, 'Hey Kevin, that was a tough one, huh?' He'd be totally honest about it. There'd be some guys who came into the program, and their parents would show up and say, 'We came a long way; you had that team down by 10 points, and you didn't put our son in for one minute.' Or they'd tell Kevin how to coach. The players would say, 'Dad, don't do that; you're making my life miserable; you're killing me!' One guy's girlfriend would even call into Kevin's radio show after the games!"

## Beating Kentucky to Get to the Sweet 16

McIlvaine: "Well, it's one of the few weapons I've got against other NBA players. I've always got the upper hand on Rex Chapman and Kenny Walker when I see them. I saw Walker at a golf outing in Cincinnati. Kenny's cart was next to mine. I wrote down on a bunch of different pieces of paper, 'Marquette owns Kentucky!' I gave them to my caddy and said, 'Tuck one of those into each pocket of Kenny's bag.'

"That year, Kentucky, earlier in the season, had been down something like 30 points to LSU, and they came back and won that game. The thing I remember most; we came into halftime and had a pretty good lead on them. I don't know if Kevin brought it up, or anybody brought it up. We came back out for the second half, and we were warming up; we were serious.

"Then we said, 'Where's the Kentucky guys? How come they're not out here yet?'

"We figured maybe coach [Rick] Pitino's yelling at them. When they finally did come out, right before the start of the second half; they were kind of lackadaisical.

"We said, 'Man, if our coach yelled at us like I think he would for a first half like that, we wouldn't come out and warm up for the second half like they're warming up. They just don't care, or they think they're going to come back and beat us like they did LSU. We just have to make sure that doesn't happen.'

"It was almost like we got motivated more, just watching them warm up for that minute and a half. It seemed like an insult, like they didn't take us seriously. They thought they were going to come back and beat us. That's what I remembered most about that game. They were seeded higher than we were. It's one of those things where this is a real big name school. This isn't Bethune-Cookman or one of those first-round patsies. I thought, 'This is our chance to beat a really big-name team, and we were looking forward to it.'

"It seemed like we were doing all this stuff that Kevin said we could do. When he recruited us, he made up these fake newspaper headlines, like, 'McIlvaine takes down Mourning. Marquette takes down Georgetown.' He'd change it around for everybody. For Robb it'd be, 'Logterman outguns Chris Jackson. Marquette beats LSU.'

"Once O'Neill got his guys there, we knew it was like, 'Okay, now you've got everything like you want it; it's time to get serious.' We knew we were going to turn around and really kick it in at that point. We did have the feeling our first year there that we were in transition. We were working hard, but it was kind of a throwaway season for us."

## Never Late For K.O.—Or Else!

McIlvaine: "There was the time that Robb and I missed the bus to go the shootaround at Kobo Hall. We were playing Detroit-Mercy. We were only a block away. The two of us had to run over there and pretty much break into the building to get there on time."

## Mac's Fondest Memory

McIlvaine: "Even more than the Kentucky game, for me was the trip to Australia. Kevin said he wanted to go over there, because, 'They speak English there; you can buy a hamburger there.' We went to Sydney and Melbourne. Then we went to Fiji.

"A lot of guys went bungee jumping, not me! I don't think Damon [Key] did, either. He was afraid of heights. We went to this place where they had a crane set up in the harbor on the marina. The crane was over the water. They said, 'We've got special cords for you guys.' Damon and I looked at each other like, 'Yeah right, sure you do!' It looked like if something happened, if you snapped your neck with that crane, you'd be gone, never to be found again! So we passed on that. We wanted no part of that!"

## Asleep on the Bus

McIlvaine: "That was a really good, good trip. We really bonded as a team. One time, though, it might have been in Melbourne, we got on the bus. It had beds in the back. I fell asleep in there. Everybody got off the bus except me. I woke up; my Walkman was on the floor; my batteries were rolling on the floor. I was rolling all over the floor. The bus was going like 80 miles an hour, weaving in and out of traffic—and there was nobody else on it! The guys just wanted to get off and go to the clubs. They forgot all about me!

"The bus driver found me and said, 'It's a good thing you woke up when you did; because another 10 minutes, and you would have been spending the night at my house!'

"He turned around and came back. I got back to the hotel. That had been enough time for everybody else to get upstairs and shower to go out for the night.

"The guys saw me and said, 'Why are you still in your gear? Aren't you coming out?'

"I said, 'Thanks for waking me up!'"

## A Fight in New Zealand and Playing in Fiji

McIlvaine: "We got into a fight, probably the biggest fight I've ever been in on the basketball court. We were playing a New Zealand team that wasn't very good. They had a couple fiery guards; they were getting waxed. One of the referees looked like he was 14 years old. The New Zealand coaches were screaming at the ref. Kevin was doing his normal thing. That young ref looked like he was starting to cry. He'd had enough. He just left. I'd never seen that happen before.

"There was a fight. One of their players' moms came out of the stands with a program. She was attacking Kevin with it! The cops showed up. We just blew 'em out. We had to play them the next night. It was all over the newspaper. We got a call from the American embassy.

"They said, 'If you get into another fight, we're not going to let you leave the country.'

"We had a little time that day to go around and sightsee. I wanted to get a sheepskin rug. We had our Marquette warmups on. People were looking at us like we'd just shot their dog! We thought, 'OK, let's just play this game and get out of here.' We beat them by 45 points. Kevin made a point of saying, 'We're going to bury them and bury them good.' We did.

"Then we got up to Fiji, which was kind of like a reward for the whole trip. We won every game. We knew that we were going to beat Fiji, because half the guys in our clinic before the game were people we played against!

"The court was the worst basketball court I've ever seen in my life. You could barely see the lines because of the dirt that was all over it. There was some guy going around before the game, pulling nails out of the court, pounding nails back in.

"They were wearing Michigan State gear, from when State came in a couple years earlier. You slid all over the court because of all that dirt. Kevin pulled all the starters after 10 minutes. He put a number on the manager's back and put him in there. He didn't want to hurt any of his key players. We were clearly better than they were. But then, at the end of the game he said, 'Let them score some points so the guys in New Zealand will see it.' We only beat them by 10 after we beat New Zealand by 45."

## Big Mac Makes It to the Pros

McIlvaine: "That was always the thing about basketball for me. In high school, Kevin Rankin was on my AAU team, Damon Key and all those guys. Kevin knew what was going to happen to me.

Ric Cobb grabbed 545 rebounds in only two seasons for the Warriors.
*From the Marquette University Department of Special Collections and University Archives*

Damon knew, but I didn't know. They said, 'You're going to make it. You're going to be in the NBA.' Ric Cobb would say, 'If you really loved the game, you'd be a lottery pick; you'd be an NBA All-Star.' I enjoyed it. I really loved the competitive aspect of it, but I wasn't like Robb [Logterman], where I wanted to lock myself in a gym and never come out. But even in high school, I'd say, 'Well, what if I blow my knee out; what if something happens? I was just going for the education. Everything else was gravy after that.'

"[Former Marquette assistant] Craig McMillan gave me some advice. I think he was talking to a scout for the Timberwolves.

"He said, 'Ya gotta stop talking about water skiing. It scares the scouts. They wonder how serious you are about the game.'

"I said, 'Alright.'

"It wasn't as if I was going out of my way to talk about it. People asked me questions.

"McMillan said, 'Stop talking about it; change the subject. Keep your haircut short; stay pale in the summer; don't talk about water skiing. Let everybody know you're serious about basketball.'"

## Big Mac's Success

McIlvaine: "I think a lot of it is attributable to Kevin and Ric. Those two guys really made me realize what was available to me out there, how far I could really take it. They had connections and knew the scene a little bit better. The places they took me, the exposure they got me, really opened my eyes. Assistants such as Craig McMillan, Bo [Ellis], and Dan Theiss, they reminded me that it wasn't a short trip; it was a long journey. Sometimes, little bumps come in the road. But they told me, I wouldn't even remember in two months. They were right. Two months later, when I was heaving in a garbage can, they said, 'You don't even remember two months ago when you thought your ankle had fallen off when we were running these sprints.' They always helped put it in perspective. It was smart of Kevin to surround himself with people who had that firsthand experience. Craig played at Arizona, and Bo played at

George Thompson (left), Jim McIlvaine (center), and Steve "The Homer" True (right) chat during a radio broadcast. Years later, McIlvaine would join them in the booth for a few games as an analyst.
*From the Marquette University Department of Special Collections and University Archives*

Marquette. Bo knew what it was like to get to the next level and play in the NBA. The best head coaches seem to surround themselves with good assistants. When Kevin was an assistant and I was playing against him in the pros, I'd go over and talk to him. He'd come over and talk to me. Once I stopped playing, I kind of lost touch with him. But my number hasn't changed since college."

## Big Mac Now

Jim McIlvaine lives in his native Wisconsin, with his wife and two children. He is a man of many talents, from photography to writing (McIlvaine is an auto racing buff) to scuba diving. McIlvaine joined Steve True and George Thompson in the radio booth for a few Marquette games during the 2004-2005 season. He was named the new color analyst for the 2005-2006 season. He replaced George Thompson, who retired after 27 years in the booth. McIlvaine is enjoying the good life. Best of all, he's still the same humble gentleman he was, coming out of Racine's St. Catherine's High School.

# CHAPTER 10

# Mike Deane

The native of Stony Point, New York, Mike Deane took the reins of the Marquette basketball team in 1994 after Kevin O'Neill left to become the head coach at the University of Tennessee. Deane had been the head coach at Siena College in Loudonville, New York, from 1986 to 1994. Right before he came to Marquette, Deane's 1994 Siena Saints had made it to the Final Four of the NIT.

While at Marquette, Deane guided the Golden Eagles to a 100-55 record in five seasons. Under Deane's leadership, the Golden Eagles had four 20-win seasons, won the 1997 Conference USA Championship tournament, and were runners-up at the 1995 NIT. His first four teams at Marquette ranked in the top 10 in the NCAA in scoring defense and field goal-percentage defense.

After a rough fifth season where the Eagles went 14-15 and failed to make a postseason tournament (the only time that happened during his tenure), Deane was fired by Marquette. After a stopover in Texas as head coach at Lamar, Deane is now the coach at Wagner University in New York.

## Why Marquette?

Deane: "Well, I had been at Siena for eight years. During that time, we had gone to three NITs and one NCAA Tournament. Each

Mike Deane led Marquette to 100 wins during his five years on the bench.
*From the Marquette University Department of Special Collections and University Archives*

of those years, there were opportunities for me to leave, but I didn't think they were the right opportunities at the right time. I really loved the job at Siena.

"I thought that of all the jobs I had been offered over the years, the Marquette job was the closest parallel to Siena, but at the top level of college basketball. It had a high academic tradition and obviously a rich basketball tradition. When Kevin [O'Neill] went to Tennessee, Dan Theiss, who'd been my assistant at Siena before he came to Marquette with Kevin, was a connection. So was [then-Marquette women's head coach] Jim Jabir, who'd coached our women's program at Siena. I had been there a few times. I knew a lot about the program. We had just finished a run to the Final Four in the NIT at Siena College, which was a very strong accomplishment. I had been talking with Dayton about that job.

Then I had a contact with [athletic director Bill] Cords. Dayton had shown strong interest in me after the NIT. I was confident that they were going to offer me the job there. I said, 'If Marquette was interested, they would have to show that quickly.' A few days after the NIT ended, I came back and had two offers. I had a decision to make.

"Dan Theiss was at Marquette; Jim Jabir was at Marquette, and I knew the young talent there from recruiting in the area. I'd seen the Marquette players, and they were very, very talented. In the end, my final decision was really based on the strength of the players, because I liked both places and both athletic directors. Because Dan was going to stay with me and because I knew Jim and had always had a very positive working relationship with him, it kind of swung the tide to go to Marquette."

## Goals and Hopes at Marquette

Deane: "I thought that Marquette at that time had a chance to be a high academic choice of upper-level Division I guys in the Midwest. I had always felt that Notre Dame had a bit of a ride during the Digger Phelps era. But I didn't think they were real strong in basketball during my time at Marquette. I thought that we'd be a parallel to Siena, a private Catholic school that attracted the players I had been used to coaching. I felt the great tradition, fan support, and interest in the community—despite a pro team being in town—would be pluses.

"I wanted to be the best basketball team we could be without sacrificing character or academic preparedness for talent. That's always been my approach. I had a great deal of success graduating players, particularly the ones I recruited, on time. I felt Marquette was a place where I could continue to do that. We had success there doing that. We also won some basketball games along the way."

## Run to NIT Championship Game

Deane: "I remember the game against South Florida with a very controversial call that sent the game to overtime. Fortunately, South Florida only made one of two foul shots. We won that game in overtime. I remember the fans storming the court at the arena [now the U.S. Cellular Arena]. They had a Frank Sinatra tape, with him singing 'New York, New York' in the background. Everyone was really excited. If you get to the Final Four of the NIT, it's a fun place to be. It's not like the NCAA, where everybody has to wear a badge and somebody's checking on it every 17 feet when you're walking. The NIT really treats the four teams very, very well.

"We had a very difficult game in the semifinals [against Penn State], which we won by using a press that we hadn't used all season. We got into the final game [against Virginia Tech]. Unfortunately, we lost that one at the buzzer [in overtime]. They hit two free throws with no time on the clock to win.

"I think I'm the only guy who ever brought two schools to the finals of the NIT in back-to-back years. That team, my first year at Marquette, was a lot of fun."

## 100 Wins in Five Years—Consistency

Deane: "Marquette is a place where basketball is a top priority. There's no football. Yet there's a quality sports program there overall. There are a lot of good coaches there. I'm still friends with a lot of them. You had resources at the time. Unfortunately, from a recruiting standpoint, the Old Gym was not a very attractive place. The locker room situation wasn't the best. I think what they have now was the right step that they needed to make to take it to an even higher level on a more consistent basis. Certainly [the Al McGuire Center], although I haven't seen it, is reported to be just what was needed at Marquette University.

"I come back to Milwaukee two or three times a year. I play in a benefit golf outing every year. I have a lot of friends. I probably have more of my closest friends in Milwaukee than anyplace else. I have a very good relationship with the guys at the booster club [at Marquette] and still maintain that relationship with almost all of them.

"Marquette was a fun time, an exciting time, a pressure-packed time. It was an opportunity to coach at the highest level of college basketball. I've always been appreciative of that opportunity. I'll never say that I agree with their decision to make a change, but I know they have the right to make that. I root for Tom [Crean] and his program. I did while he had some of my players. Now that he doesn't and he's doing very well, I'm very happy for him. Tom and I were good friends prior to his coming to Marquette. I have very strong feelings for Marquette University and the opportunities they gave me. Like I said, it was a fun five years."

## Deane's Dream Run in
## 1996-1997 C-USA Tourney

Deane: "We won four games in 72 hours, 78 hours, something like that. That was a great stretch for us. That was an exciting weekend to say the least. At the time, we were only the second school that had done it. Since then, a number of other schools have done it. We ended up with a pretty hot team that year. Unfortunately, we kind of ran out of gas because of the strain it took on us on the weekend before the start of the NCAA Tournament."

(MU lost to Providence, 81-59 in round one of the NCAA.)

"We had played in the conference tourney on Thursday night; we finished on Sunday morning. We beat DePaul, Memphis, Cincinnati, and Charlotte. There was a lot of talent. I think it was great for the Marquette program. It was very good for [Marquette's leading scorer] Chris Crawford's career, because it got him a little notoriety. That was great; it was fun, too."

Chris Crawford's foul problems against Providence in the 1997 NCAA Tournament added to Mike Deane's frustrations, which eventually bubbled over and led to Deane's early exit from the game.

*From the Marquette University Department of Special Collections and University Archives*

# Deane's Temper Tantrum in
# NCAA Loss to Providence

Deane: "The Providence game, what happened was we were just in the middle of making whatever run we were going to make. We had cut the deficit to 14. Anthony Pieper was going in for a lay-in. There was a foul; [the officials] didn't call a foul. Anthony missed the lay-in. Chris Crawford went over the back and got his fifth foul. That pretty much ended our chances. Anthony had a cut from the top of his forehead to his eye and from the side of his face down to his lip. I was disappointed that the foul wasn't called. But that wasn't really why I was involved in the controversy. That controversy was over the blood rule, where they were saying Anthony had to come out.

"I said, 'Well, wait a minute, you fouled my guy out; you didn't call a foul here!'

"Regrettably, I got a little bit out of control there. I overstepped my bounds, and the officials handled it well. They knew what they had to do, unfortunately. I should have walked away after the first technical—and didn't. As a matter of fact, I remember telling the official, 'Well, if you didn't see the foul, I don't see the cut!' That didn't sit too well with him. It might have been funny the first time it came out; by the third time, he had no choice but to eject me. That was a frustrating game for us. We were so tired from the league tournament. We played well in the first eight minutes, and then, as I said, we were starting to make that one run in the second half. If we were going to do anything, we needed Chris on the floor. It was a combination of frustration—it wasn't really so much that they didn't call the foul, but more the way the thing unfolded. We lost our best player on the fifth foul because they didn't call the foul. Then they were going to take my next best player out of the game because he had a cut.

"[The cut] wasn't going to be easy to clean up. He had a fingernail wide cut from the top of his forehead all the way down his face. If you remember, they made a shot from the opposite foul line at the end of the half. So everything they were putting up was going in. That was regrettable, but it wasn't like that was a commonplace occurrence. While I'm an emotional guy on the floor, into every facet of all the games, I didn't get a lot of technical fouls. That was just one of those things that happened.

"When I think of the great coaches who have gotten thrown out of the NCAA, unfortunately, they have to mention me with them. But the names are pretty good, Dean Smith and Al McGuire are on that list. I'm sure when it was all said and done that neither of them was happy that it happened. It didn't hurt my team's chances; that's the good thing about it. But when you represent the university, you want to do that in a positive way. In hindsight, I wish that hadn't happened, but it did."

## Impact of MU Experience on Deane

Deane: "Marquette was different than any other place I've coached. I still talk to a lot of the guys who played for me. I have close relationships with them. When the Final Four was in Atlanta, Chris Crawford called me with Mike Bargen. I had them out until 4:30 a.m. Needless to say, we had a few Coca Colas! To see how well all those guys are doing, that's why I coach. I like to win games, but it's not an end in itself. Marquette was, at the time for me, a very lucrative opportunity. In hindsight, do I have any regrets about making that move? No. However, sometimes when you're asked to step down after you've won 100 games in five years, and you're starting three freshmen, you get a little concerned about what people are going to think. Other than that, I didn't coach any different at Marquette than I did at Siena or at Oswego State, or Lamar after that, or here now at Wagner. The difference at Marquette was that you had more resources than you need, actually.

"You also had very, very high expectations. But you want to be at a program that has high expectations. Marquette was certainly one that was well known to players. Recruiting was a challenge there because you played top schools. But you didn't have to try hard to figure out which kid was going to get better. That's what you had to do at Siena; that's what you had to try to do at Lamar or Wagner. You have to take guys—you don't reload at places like this. You have to try to rebuild. That's exactly what we're trying to do now, especially when we've got seven healthy players. I've had to practice with them myself to have enough guys the last 13 or 14 practices. I can do all right, as long as we're in the halfcourt. We haven't been running much because I could get killed out there! It's been a tough year. We had four guards go down, two starters and our starting small forward. But in two more years, I think we can be very good here and have a chance to win the league.

"I'm not one of these guys who wants to coach until he's 75. There'll be a time for me to step away from it. When I do, the one thing I hope we have is a big party. A big reunion where players from everyplace that I've coached come back, and we'll sit around and tell lies. That's one thing I want to have happen when I step aside. I'm 53; I'm not ready to quit yet. Again, I'm not going to coach until I'm 75; that's never been an ambition of mine. I'm going to work a little while longer."

## MU to The Big East

Deane: "Tom [Crean] has always been forward thinking and ambitious. The next logical step [after Conference USA] was to get involved with the move to The Big East, if they wanted to stay at the top level. That's what they want to do; that's what they're committed to doing. So, I can't see what other alternative they really have. I still believe that somewhere down the road, maybe not before my career is over, there is a Catholic School League that is going to evolve. That's going to include Midwestern schools like DePaul, Marquette, St. Louis, and Xavier, with the non football-playing eastern schools like Villanova, St. John's, and Georgetown. They may even go as far as Temple, those kinds of schools. I think that at some point in time that evolutionary process is going to place, but for now, I think it's an inventive move for Marquette. It certainly means a lot more travel. I say that—but not really—because there was only one bus ride in Conference USA, and that was the DePaul game. Everything else was a plane ride.

"I'm not sure it made that much difference from that perspective. I just think it's always difficult when you're on one geographic end of any league. That was the case in Conference USA, and that's the case in The Big East. You're always a little bit farther out than a lot of schools are. They're doing some things now, spending some money that they weren't spending when I was there. They try to reduce the stress and strain; they're chartering [planes] a lot more, and they're doing a lot of things. So, I think they're well prepared to go into The Big East."

## Recruiting in The Big East

Deane: "I always felt Penn State started to slide when they went to the Big Ten, where they didn't have an identity. They had a name, but no recognition in terms of those recruiting areas. Whereas Marquette, the players in the state of Wisconsin have gotten better and better. There seems to be enough guys in the Wisconsin, Illinois, Minnesota, and Michigan areas to take care of the Big Ten and Big East schools. Everybody that's really good in Conference USA is going to The Big East. I think it'll be a very competitive league. There are some ambitious schools, but I think it's the right move for Marquette. I think they would have been left out. They didn't want to settle for the Atlantic 10, I'm sure. That would have been a move backward. Every move they've made over the last 15 to 20 years in the evolution of the program has been forward."

## What Did You Try to Instill in Your Players?

Deane: "The one thing people always say is that our teams work very, very hard, especially on the defensive end. We were a relatively smart team because on paper, athletically, we didn't always match up. But we always seemed to be able to beat a lot of teams with more athletic ability—not necessarily basketball talent—but athletic ability. I always try to teach the guys that the program and the team are more important than the individual.

"If people wanted to make a change, there was no sense worrying about that. I had to worry about myself at the time. The program was bigger than me; it was bigger than the individuals. I tried to get the guys to get the most out of—I hoped they had a well-rounded experience, socially, academically, and athletically. I tried to teach guys to have a balance between the three. When it's basketball season, basketball raises up a little bit higher on the scale. The rest of the year, I really wanted them to concentrate harder on their schoolwork.

"Everybody I recruited at Marquette graduated in May of his last year of eligibility, even the guys who had transferred. Those guys all graduated on time; I was very proud of that. They're all doing exceptionally well, a lot better than you and I are doing! Bart Miller is an architect in Pittsburgh. He got his master's degree at MIT. In fact, they named the academic award in athletics at Marquette for him. He is a great kid. Amal [McCaskill] and Chris [Crawford] are still playing. Chris is hurt, of course. Amal was in the league.

"How about this? Here's the irony of the coaching world. I had a player, Nigel Wyatt, last year. He was first-team all-league here. He was playing for a team in Belgium. The team loses its point guard, guess who they sign? Tony Miller. So now Nigel and Tony are playing together, and they're in first place in the league.

"I always felt that your team should mirror, as best it can, the general student population. I remember, when I got to Marquette, the first nine or 10 guys they had were all communications majors. Not that there's anything wrong with that. Then when I got there, things changed. The majority of the guys were in business. John Polonowski was in physical therapy; Bart Miller and John Mueller were in engineering. They ended up being in places around campus that not everybody expected of basketball players. I've tried to do that on every campus I've been at. Obviously everybody did well at Marquette. Everybody graduated when I coached at Lamar. So far everybody has graduated from Wagner. That's a big part of my job.

Teaching is a big part of my job. I think the biggest part of the job is to balance the experience for the players, so that they get the most out of their potential—academically and athletically, and then they can develop personally. Think back to when you were 18 and how much different you were from 21 or 22. I have to kind of oversee the development of a group of guys who in some ways are exposed to more and in other ways are sheltered. You have to be careful. Certainly when you hit the top level like Marquette, those guys travel all over the country. They've experienced a lot before they come to school. A lot of people are taking care of them along the way. You have to teach them that you're going to get out of the experience what you put into it."

# CHAPTER 11

# Tom Crean

**N**obody in his right mind could have foreseen Marquette making it back to the Final Four. But nobody could have foreseen how special a coach Tom Crean would become. With the magnificent Dwyane Wade, Crean led MU to college basketball's greatest showcase in April 2003.

Unlike some of his predecessors, who tried to keep a distance from the McGuire legacy, and the huge shadow it cast, current MU coach Tom Crean welcomed the legend with open arms. Al felt comfortable coming around and offering his considerable wisdom. In the 18 months before Al's death, the two men developed a close and unique relationship.

## How He Made You Feel

Crean: "Most people who were around him, and I got a year and a half, you couldn't do justice to how he made you feel. The memories are vivid, and they're vivid because I don't want to lose them. My wife said it best.

"'He makes you feel better about you than you could ever make him feel about himself.'

"That was especially true when he was sick near the end. All you can do is try to share that, to learn from that. It's not a matter of being the next McGuire. But the way he made people feel. That's the challenge for everyone. Most of us, including me, suffer greatly if we try to compare ourselves to that. All you can do is take pieces of that and try to be aware of it. What Al did for me, he created an awareness for me about what the program was about, what more needed to be done, how his era was different. He truly gave the license to not be concerned about his time, to not live in it or dwell on it.

"The first day we were together was one of the most meaningful. I'll never forget the first time I was introduced to him. He said, 'Sometime when you have five or six hours, give me a call.' I did, and we had a great time. At the time, it was really important to me to keep all that private. I didn't think it was fair to him. I was not going to share those times, but I was learning. When he got sick, I saw him numerous times at the hospice. One of the biggest things I learned from him is that I think that man always had a plan. Where I got to watch it was how he said goodbye to everybody and how important that was to him. I'll never forget my time of saying goodbye to him. It was incredible. I remember everything about our visits. I never took any notes in front of him, but he allowed me in. To Al, it was no big deal. But to me, it was incredible. I can't even do justice to talking about that. We all have our personal memories. I think the greatest example was his funeral.

"Dick Weiss—the great writer at the New York *Daily News*— said, 'How would you sum it up in your time here?'

"I said, 'Look over there.'

"There were two people in fur coats. Here was another man who was walking in behind them into the next pew. If he had a home, he was lucky. It sounds dramatic, but it was the truth. He had an old beat-up Packers coat. The man didn't have anything. The other people who had tears streaming down their faces, there probably wasn't anything that they didn't have. Most people would never believe that story.

"I said, 'There it is, right there.'

"I didn't know those three people, but that's how he made you feel. That I'll always remember."

## Player Relationships

Crean: "I would hope that Al learned early on that my intentions were 100 percent pure. He didn't want to talk basketball. But I didn't give him a chance, especially as I started to get comfortable with him. I wanted to learn. One day during my first year, I walked into my office. He was laying on a big black chair, eating chocolate Pop-Tarts with blue jeans on, watching game film. I ended up laying on a chair, too. We talked for about an hour and a half. Eventually, I wasn't in awe. That was a great feeling. Al truly made it a friendship.

"It still affects me to think of him to this day. It's impossible to pinpoint what I learned from him. It all came back to the relationship with the players. They're all different. He knew about gamesmanship and showmanship, but there was nothing phony about the way he coached or taught or led. There were no hidden agendas. That stood out in every conversation we ever had. He was gonna fight for those players, no matter what. He was gonna discipline them and get on them and be hard on them. But nobody else was going to take shots at them. If he did, that's fine. As he said, 'Coaching's a dictatorship. You don't get to make choices on the team and on discipline. I do with you, but nobody else gets to step in and tell you how to run your team.'"

## "You'll Figure It out"

Crean: "He gave me a great piece of advice that I've never shared. There was a time in my first year when he thought I was getting spread too thin. Even to his last day he said that. I've never taken his advice to take a two-week vacation with my family where nobody can find me. Someday we will, but he said, 'It's time for you to start playing, Coach.'

"I said, 'What do you mean?'

"He said, 'You're speaking here, you're speaking there; you're doing this, you're doing that. And so and so is not playing as well as he should. It's time for you to start playing, Coach.'

"I said, 'Well ...'

"He said, 'No, no. You'll figure it out.'"

## I'm the Coach

Crean: "You're the coach, you're the coach, nobody else. He was so on target with our team. He would see things two weeks, a month before they ever happened. I had an incident with a player the first year where I thought we needed a change. He talked me right out of it. Al always had a feel. He became such a sounding board. I'd hear from him before and after every game until he got so sick that he couldn't do it. It wasn't as if he was going to tell me how to coach. He never volunteered strategy unless I asked. He never got comfortable doing it. But I'd ask enough, so we had enough conversations. That's what I took the most from him, that I'm the coach. If you lose the job someday, you make sure you lose it because you did things the way you wanted to do them. Don't listen to anybody else. You know what? He was right. And it gets harder; the more you win, the harder it gets."

## Crean's Role Models

Crean: "The person who influenced me the most would be my mom, because of the way we were raised, the times that we've gone through. She doesn't understand a lot about sports. She wasn't an athlete, but when it comes to trusting you and giving you an opportunity to follow your dreams and giving you guidance, she was No. 1. She gave of herself so much in raising my sister and me. She gave so much to other people. Mom was such a great role model. She never held us back; it would have been real easy to become stagnant, to hold back. Mom gave me confidence. She told me to choose what I wanted to do; that's what was so special. She empowered me.

"The other person who influenced me the most was Jack Harbaugh. He's been so much more than a father-in-law. As a fine coach, [Harbaugh led the Western Kentucky football team to the 2002 NCAA Division I-AA Championship in his final season], he taught me about running a team and dealing with the frustration. A coach is in the middle of so many situations; yet he can't stay in the middle ground. What an outsider's view of a coach's balance and what actually is balance are two entirely different things. You have to connect your family to everything you do. It's my job to understand what my role is. That's why I have it in my contract that my family can travel with me. [Athletic director] Bill Cords allows that. I couldn't imagine what it'd be like without that. Family being together in basketball is important. You won't necessarily win a lot more games that way, but you sure could lose a lot. When you have disconnection, you lean on family. They're gonna come up. You've got to keep connecting the dots all the time. Every dot is unbelievably important."

## Meeting Joani

Crean: "I was living in Bowling Green, Kentucky, coaching at Western Kentucky.

"A man by the name of Steve Small, who was assistant coach for the women's team at the time, said, 'You're in here all the time; you gotta be sleeping here. You need to go out and do something, or you're going to get sick.'

"I said, 'Yeah, I can run around here, or I can go down to the track.'

"He said, 'No, you need a health club. I'm gonna have somebody give you a call about a health club.'

"This was in August 1990.

"So I get a call from Joani. I knew the name right away. Of course, I knew her dad, but I hadn't met him yet. She was sales director for Lover's Lane Health and Racquet Club.

"She said, 'I'd like to have you see it.'

"So I said, 'Sometime maybe I will.'

"I called her one time.

"I said, 'You know, I'm going to get a chance to come out.'

"It's after the recruiting period.

"She said, 'Great.'

"So I get out there and I see her, and it was an incredible feeling. I'll never forget. She wore a white polo shirt, peach shorts, and tennis shoes. She walked right up to the counter. I was awestruck. She showed me around the health club, which was impressive. But when I left, I thought there was no way I'd have time to join.

"I went back to the office. I was working with a guy named Charles Cunningham, who was an assistant coach with me.

"I said, 'You're not going to believe this. I just met the girl I'm going to marry!'

"It was truly one of those things. He was the only one who heard that.

"Joani and I didn't make any plans to date at that point. We didn't start getting together until the next year. We'd see each other around a little bit. She was starting to get the inkling that I liked her. But I was involved in other things; so was she. I was in another relationship, but it was long distance."

In between studying game tapes and preparing to become a head coach, Crean made his decision, and the two were married. The couple now has three beautiful young children.

## What Crean Saw in Marquette

Crean: "I'd been a Marquette fan a long time. My first memories of really paying attention to basketball were with that 1977 team. I remember bits and pieces of that national championship game. But I was like most kids; television wasn't as huge yet for college basketball. I was a diehard Central Michigan fan."

(Crean grew up in Mount Pleasant, Michigan.)

"Marquette was the team I paid attention to on a national scope. Then Michigan State won a national championship."

Tom Crean cheers on his Golden Eagles squad.
*From the Marquette University Department of Special Collections and University Archives*

(Magic Johnson's Spartans beat Larry Bird's Indiana State Sycamores in 1979.).

"Then I became hooked on the game.

"I got to know [former Marquette coach] Kevin O'Neill. I knew what the program stood for. I always held it in the highest regard. The tradition of the program, coming from Michigan State, I knew what that was all about. Being in the Midwest was really important to me at that point. I knew I wasn't necessarily going to stay in Michigan. But I wanted to stay in the Midwest for family reasons.

"Once I got here, seeing all the great things that were here, I took the job. I didn't even know we had dorms like we had. I'd been to the Bradley Center; I'd been to the Old Gym. It didn't bother me one bit.

"They asked me, 'What do you think about our facilities?' It was like they were apologizing.

"I said, 'Well, it has eight baskets; that's a good sign to me.'

"I grew up in that landscape. That's why the McGuire Center is like a Taj Mahal. But I don't want it to be where we won't continue to get down and dirty to do the work we need to get done. We roll up the sleeves and go at it; that's the way it's gotta be.

"What really sold the job for me was the people I met early on: [athletic director] Bill Cords, [Jesuit] Andy Thon, and [Marquette president] Father Wild. They were really huge. It was a no-brainer for me. I wanted it. Once I realized they wanted me, I wanted it even more. It wasn't like I played hard to get. I wanted to come. It was great."

## Student Involvement

Crean: "I don't think you can win without it. You've always got to find what the winning edge is. There's a lot of winning edges. You've got to be able to find them. You're not going to win anything without fans behind you. When it became public that I was involved in this job, two Conference USA coaches that I asked told me there was no home-court advantage in the Bradley Center. A third volunteered it. Before I ever came in, I knew what the perception was on the outside. That was one issue. The other was embracing the Marquette tradition again. I had two rising juniors in my office for an unofficial visit. Seventeen pictures of former players hung on the walls. They could only identify three or four. People had forgotten all about the tradition. Cincinnati was the only home game that drew students. My past was probably the biggest thing in helping me. I was around when Dan Majerle starred at Central Michigan. The students used to throw toilet paper on the floor after the first basket. It became a national thing. It took 10 to 15 minutes to remove it, to the point where officials started calling technical fouls. It was incredible. When I was at Michigan State with Tom Izzo, the students had the Iz-Zone.

"The Green Bay Packers also came into play for me. I had read the book *The Packer Way* by Ron Wolf."

(Wolf guided the Packers to two straight Super Bowls. The Packers won the 1997 Super Bowl.)

"When I got the job, I went back and reread it. There were similarities between Wolf inheriting the Packers, and the great tradition that the fans had forgotten about.

"So I went to work marketing the program. One idea was: Coffee, Crean, and Doughnuts. Only 40 people showed up at the first one. I had all the players there. I'd been so excited. I went home depressed. But I looked back the next day and said, 'Man, those 37 people are gonna become mouthpieces for what we want to do.'

"We had to change the culture. The students didn't feel connected with the players. Being at a game wasn't the 'in' thing to do. Walking the dog was about as big an event, unless Cincinnati was in town. There was an apathy, but nobody was to blame. My first year, we had 300 to 400 students in there. [During 2003-2004 season] we have 5,000. Once you've hit it like we have, with attendance records like we have, you've got to take it up another step. And there's no room to rest. Sometimes people think, once you've built it, you can take a rest. You can't do that. That's been the whole mindset the entire time.

"We don't have football. When you're responsible for what goes on with the other sports financially, what goes into the other sports financially, and what goes on with money coming into the school in an athletic sense, you either blow it or you take it real, real seriously. There's no middle ground."

## Dwyane Wade

Crean: "I don't think anybody ever thought he'd be as good as he is, as good as he was. I'd be lying if I said we thought he could be that good that fast. Even when he was here the first year, you knew he was going to be good.

"It was June 21, I spoke with Dwyane on the phone for 25 minutes. I'll never forget it as long as I live. There was just something about him. You could just tell. That started the connection. I had a lot of feeling for him before I ever saw him play. You can have that feeling for people and then as soon as you see them play, they're not good enough. As soon as you saw Dwyane play, you knew the athleticism was there. He was a guy who wasn't ranked in the top 500 high school players going into his senior season. He wasn't invited to Nike camp. Twelve other players in the Chicagoland area were. He was the fifth option on his AAU team. He played with guys like Darius Miles, T.J. Cummings, Matt Lottich, and Odartey Blankson. They were better basketball players at that point. But he had that athleticism. You'd see it once, and you'd say, 'Wow! He's got a chance to do that all the time.' You'd see flashes of his brilliance; his brilliance became his passion and his patience. Great players have a sense of urgency, but they have a patience that goes along with that. It's hard to describe, but Dwyane's got that. He always had that. It just didn't always show up. Being here at Marquette helped out because the one thing he didn't come with was confidence. We knew after we signed him that we had somebody pretty good based on a day in high school when he had 48 points and 12 rebounds at 10 a.m., and 42 and 17 at 8 p.m.

"We knew we had somebody who was really, really good, and there weren't a lot of schools on him. DePaul kind of messed around him and laid behind the academics. Illinois State recruited him really, really hard. St. Louis tinkered with him. The thing that finally sold him was we agreed to take him even if he didn't qualify [with test scores]. We made the commitment, and thank God Father Wild stuck with me on it. Because then Dwyane knew he wasn't going to be abandoned.

"One of the proudest things was he left here with a 2.8 GPA in his final semester. Other players in his position of getting drafted were dropping out of school left and right. You could see some real qualities as a person in Dwyane. The playing just took off, but he worked. It was not uncommon for him the night before a game to stay in the gym after meetings ended at 9:30 p.m. or 10 p.m. and shoot. It wasn't required, but there he'd be. He'd shoot 500 or 600 shots a day after a Miami Heat practice in his rookie year. That's why he's not even scratching the surface as to what kind of player he's going to be. As a human being, as a husband, as a father, you'd be hard-pressed to find any negatives."

## Crean's Players

Crean: "What I've learned about this is it's a two-way street. I don't know if it's the way I was brought up. I don't know if it was the people who affected me. It's probably the way I was brought up. There is a feeling you have for your players that you really can't turn on and off. You don't want to turn it on and off. I'm affected by bad practices. I'm really affected by bad behavior. I'm affected by bad choices because you want so much more for them. If it's heartfelt, they know it. But as a coach, it needs to be heartfelt back. As a coach, the connection you build with your players; that should never go away if it's meaningful. I wouldn't have understood that as an assistant or even a first- or second-year head coach. I understand it big time now. If you've got their best interests in mind, you can't waver from it. You can't change the standards that you've set, and you've got to keep helping them raise the standards. Every coach and player is accountable, and the head coach has to make sure that he's holding everyone accountable. We've got some real unique two-way streets running through here, and that's a lot of fun. One-way streets aren't a lot of fun at all, and they're not lasting. You're always trying to build with your core people and your players. That's the best.

"We're getting closer to that all the time. I've learned so much about leadership, but I've learned so much more about the legacy of leadership. That begins when they leave. Anybody who says you're going to have the same relationship with everybody—that's not accurate. That's true in any walk of life, but the two-way streets, you can't ever get enough of that. I'm trying to understand that."

## Final Four Season Memories

Crean: "Great teams are close. But like any family, you're going to have disagreements and issues. There'll be guys who won't bring it certain days. The thing that stood out the most about that team was the forgiveness, me as a coach included. I didn't stay mad for long or carry things around. The reason we won is because we didn't have problems. We did a thing at the beginning of the year. I said, 'We can be a team of destiny if we really want to be. We had a great taste of it last year [2001-2002]. But to do that, we really have to be a family. We cannot have problems.'

"We had a thing called 90-10. What that meant was if 90 percent of our focus and energy is on ourselves and getting better and only 10 percent on adversity and distractions and not getting along, we can win.

"I said, 'If we can get this thing to 95-5, we can get to New Orleans. If the thing is 80-20, we may not be in the top three in the league. If it gets to 70-30 or 60-40, we may not have a winning season. We have a superstar [Dwyane Wade]. That's just the way that it is. If he starts acting like one, then we don't have a superstar anymore. We have a new guy, who's never played at this level [six-foot-10 Robert Jackson] who can take us a long way. (I say never at this level, even though he was third-team All-SEC, because he had never guarded anybody.)'

"It was amazing how few problems we had. Anytime something came up, there was automatic forgiveness. We never stagnated. There was a real hunger to get better. There was no comfort level on the team that year. There was a comfort level with each other, but not with the play. As a leader and a group, you want to be secure and connected. Dwyane and Rob brought security to everyone. I think we'll remember that team for so many years, because the standard they set was so unbelievable. There were no personal agendas. In this day and age, that's the toughest thing for a coach. There's a culture out there that's a real challenge for any coach. But I wouldn't want to do anything else because the thrill of it—you just can't replace."

## The Origin of the Superdome Picture During the Final Four Season

Crean: "I don't know what triggered it. But it was really about seeing it before we could ever really achieve it. It was an out-there thing. But I thought we needed that. We'd recovered from guys transferring; we had a great spring and summer. Everybody's work ethic went up. The camaraderie started to build.

"Late in the summer I said to [assistant] Trey Schwab, 'Let's get a shot of the Superdome, not a football shot, but let's try to get a dome shot.'

"Trey got it. We had it blown up. I introduced it before the second exhibition game my fourth year. I put it on the board. I said, 'Let's set a standard.' We did that. Scott Merritt was the first one to sign it. Eventually, everybody did. We got it framed. We took it everywhere. It didn't leave the locker room unless we did. It went on the road. We'd wrap it up and take it like tape and shoes. When we went to Tulane, Trey and I got a guy who was running the Superdome. I had the bus driver take us a different route. The guys eventually took notice. We stopped at the dome.

"And I said, 'Before we can achieve it, we've got to see it, and we've got to believe it. That's what we're going to spend the next 30 minutes doing.'

"We all got out and filed in there. There was no turf down or no courts, just cement.

"I asked the man, 'Can you show us center court? Can you show us where the benches will be?'

"The guys started running around and tossing a rubber football. We took a picture of where center court would be. I was reaching at this point, but I was trying to motivate my team. We never forgot that; that was really special."

## Holy Cross Crusaders

Crean: "It was really a challenge for me personally. I had never been in a situation as a coach where I was personally going against somebody that I had worked for [Ralph Willard, Holy Cross's coach]. So on one hand you have that personal attachment to the person you are going against, but you also know it's such a huge game for your team and for your program. Very quickly you realize you have to put your personal feelings aside and do everything you can do to put your team in position to give them the best opportunity to win, as far as what you do as a coach. The lead up to the game and the anxiety, that was the most anxious I was for any of the games, because we had not won a game yet in my time here in the NCAA Tournament. I was going against my former boss. We had a great year, and we didn't want it to end. So to me that was a huge, huge thing."

In the opening round of the 2003 NCAA Tournament, the Midwest Region's third-seeded Golden Eagles took on the Holy Cross Crusaders, the region's No. 14 seed out of the Patriot League. Sophomore guard Travis Diener suffered from insomnia the night before the game. He used his sleepless hours productively as he mentally prepared for the upcoming game. Diener lead the Golden Eagles scoring 29 points; he hit nine-of-14 shots.

The double-digit favored Golden Eagles got all they could handle from the Crusaders. With only 6:04 left in the game, Holy Cross held a 56-54 lead. Freshman guard Joe Chapman knocked down a three-pointer to give Marquette a lead they would not relinquish. The combination of Diener and All-America guard Dwyane Wade scored 13 of Marquette's final 15 points to help

Crean's crew to the 72-68 victory. The tournament win was Marquette's first since 1996 when they beat Monmouth.

The win also marked Tom Crean's first NCAA Tournament win as a head coach. He beat his friend and former boss, Ralph Willard. Willard, had given Crean his first coaching job at Western Kentucky.

## Missouri Tigers

Crean: "I recall the preparation. The preparation was one where our guys really felt that they could win that game if we did a great job on their Big Triangle, which was Arthur Johnson, Rickey Paulding, and Ricky Clemons. We felt like if we could get to those guys, we could run our sets and we could run our break. We did a great job on Ricky Clemons and Jimmy McKinney, but we didn't do a great job on Arthur Johnson and Rickey Paulding. I think that was a sign of how great they were."

Two days after narrowly defeating Holy Cross, Marquette's next opponent was the Missouri Tigers out of the Big 12 Conference. The crowd of nearly 26,000 at the RCA Dome in Indianapolis watched two promising young teams battle for a spot in college basketball's Sweet 16. Once again Marquette was led by the hot hand of Diener, who poured in 26 points. Wade battled his way through a tough shooting performance that saw him go nine for 23. Wade ended up with 24 points along with eight rebounds and seven assists.

The Golden Eagles looked to be cruising along to an easy victory as they opened up an 11-point second-half lead. The lead could be attributed to Diener, who hit four three-pointers and added a three-point play for 15 of the 19 points scored by Marquette in an amazing five-minute span.

The Tigers did not give up, kept chipping away at the lead, and tied the game at 78-78 in the closing moments. Wade knocked down a jumper from the left wing to give Marquette an 80-78 lead with 33 seconds left in the game. On the following possession,

Missouri's Arthur Johnson was fouled while backing into the post. Despite being a 55.7-percent shooter from the free throw line, Johnson knocked down both to tie the game and eventually to send it to overtime.

During the overtime, Marquette struck first as freshman Steve Novak drained a three-pointer to give Marquette the early lead. The two teams traded baskets throughout the beginning of the extra period until Novak hit another three from the left wing to give Marquette a 93-89 lead with 2:03 left in the game. Marquette then ran off eight points en route to a 101-92 victory. The victory elevated the Golden Eagles to their first trip to the Sweet 16 since 1994.

Crean: "Our guys completely stepped up throughout the game. It was a high energy game. It was a very exciting game. It was an exciting game for them to play in, and they made big plays. My memories are we came out of timeouts and had some big shots go our way. When we needed big stops, we got them. My most vivid memory was when we thought the ball was going in when Rickey Paulding shot it at the end of the game, but there was Steve Novak who gave just a little foot fake that never let Rickey get his total rhythm or get a great ride to the basket. It was just a little thing that made the whole difference of that game going into overtime. I've never been part of anything like we saw in overtime.

"I could coach 15 more years and never have a team not miss a shot in overtime with those kind of stakes."

## Pittsburgh Panthers

The Golden Eagles traveled to Minneapolis's Metrodome to take on the Midwest Regional's No. 2 seed Pittsburgh Panthers out of The Big East Conference. Up to this point, Diener's solid shooting had led Marquette to two spectacular wins.

Crean: "By this time you are really doing your best to keep it one game at a time. But your mind can play tricks on you. It's saying, 'You know what we really could be on a roll here. If we can keep it up, we could get to New Orleans.' You don't really want to prepare your team like that. You want to prepare for each and every game. Our guys knew what was at stake. They knew that if we had an opportunity to beat Pittsburgh, that we could very well see Kentucky in the next round or even Wisconsin, whom we had beaten earlier in the year." As the spotlight got brighter, All-American Dwyane Wade took control of the Golden Eagles team he had led to the Conference USA regular-season title. Despite scoring only two points in the first half, which saw Wade play sparingly due to foul problems, the guard turned it up a notch in the second half as he scored 20 of his game-high 22 points.

The Golden Eagles controlled much of the second half and looked like they were going to have an easy victory, leading 71-61 with just under four minutes left in the game. The Panthers then went on a 9-0 run to cut the lead to 71-70 with 1:30 left in the game. Junior forward Scott Merritt came up big in the closing moments of the game as he sank four free throws to give Marquette the 77-74 victory over Pittsburgh. The win put the Golden Eagles in the NCAA's Elite Eight for the first time since 1977.

Crean: "The Pittsburgh game was two teams who were really going to get after it defensively. They were going to know each other well, were very well-prepared, well-scouted teams where the players really bought into going against each other. I think we had respect for each other. What I remember most vividly about that game was the way Dwyane took over, not only with his scoring, but with his passing in the second half. So many big plays, the climatic moment at the end when Travis Diener got that ball, raised his fist, and we knew we were moving on to victory. It was a phenomenal feeling. My greatest memories are every celebration that we had, watching the team celebrate after the games, and thinking about how the bench reacted during the games. Those are fun memories."

# Kentucky Wildcats

Crean: "Before the game, the players came back into the locker room and they had a lot of life and energy. But at that point it could have been the mind playing tricks on us because we were really into that mindset of us against the world. At that point, you are looking for anything you can assume or perceive that is a slight. When you're trying to get your team into a mindset that we are really the only ones that believe that we can do this, that's where it is a lot of fun. That is exactly where our guys' mindsets were going into that game. What you are always trying to do is create a mindset, and the focus becomes what you do on a daily basis to get there. At that point, our players felt that they could play with anybody in the country. They felt they were as good as anybody in the country. We needed to be able to show that.

"I think that we got off to such a bad start, and then everybody settled down and played, and then it became like a snowball effect. It was an exciting feeling. Our players had that edge, but they had that edge going into the game where it came down to intensity, emotion, and them really believing we could win it."

In front of a crowd of 28,383 fans at the Metrodome in Minneapolis, the Marquette Golden Eagles punched their ticket to the Final Four by defeating the No. 1-ranked team in the nation, the Kentucky Wildcats. The Wildcats came into the game riding a 26-game winning streak and seemed like they were on an unstoppable path to the Final Four. That is until they ran into Dwyane Wade. Wade put on one of the greatest performances in NCAA Tournament history as he recorded his first career triple-double with 29 points, 11 rebounds, and 11 assists en route to being named most outstanding player in the Midwest Regional. Wade went over, under, around, and through Kentucky as he and the Golden Eagles shot 56.4 percent against a defense that had limited their opponents to only 41 percent shooting. This marked only the third triple-double in NCAA Tournament history as Wade joined tournament greats Andre Miller of Utah and Magic Johnson of Michigan State.

Tom Crean paces the sideline during Marquette's victoy over Kentucky in the 2003 Midwest Regional Finals.
*From the Marquette University Department of Special Collections and University Archives*

Unlike the previous three tournament appearances in which Marquette won close games, The Golden Eagles built up a huge lead against the Wildcats and never looked back. Senior center Robert Jackson added huge numbers himself with 24 points and 15 rebounds. Freshman Steve Novak also played well coming off the bench as he hit five-of-eight three pointers to finish with 16 points. The Golden Eagles seemed to score at will, and when the smoke had cleared, Marquette had an 83-69 victory in the Midwest Regional Finals.

Crean: "It doesn't sink in until it's over. There is no question that from halftime on we are thinking that if we keep this up, we have accomplished an awful lot and we have a chance to be in New Orleans. The players all knew it. It would have been silly for me to go in at halftime and act like it wasn't happening. The first thing I put up on the board was it is 0-0. We have to play with that mentality, because that's the same thing that Kentucky is going to do. We wanted to play with a 0-0 mentality, but at the same time also go back out there and play like a team that had dominated the first half and build on it. As a coach you are never comfortable. The thing for me is I remember so many moments in that game vividly. For me, that's fun because there were so many exciting parts of that game. Play by play it's easy to remember a lot of it because there were so many great ones."

## Reaching the Goal of Making It to the Final Four

Crean: "It was extremely satisfying. The thing that made it so worth it was when we walked out of the Syracuse versus Kansas game, we probably had half of our team that had tears in their eyes. They really did feel that they could have played in that game. To me that was where I knew that we really were building a program and didn't just have a team. Obviously we haven't been back since that point, but I knew we had players that truly belonged in that environment because they felt that they could have played in that game. To me that's what is satisfying about it. For me personally so much of the Final Four was a blur, but when you are able to come back and look at it, it was a great accomplishment for a lot of people, one that will be remembered at Marquette forever. For those guys, everyone that played on that team, deserves that recognition that they received for being a part of that. They did buy into a collective goal and did whatever it would take for each and everyone of them to have success. That was led by Dwyane, Robert Jackson, and Travis Diener."

## Kansas Jayhawks

A week earlier the Kentucky Wildcats had run into a brick wall called Dwyane Wade. In Marquette's first appearance in the Final Four since 1977, the Marquette Golden Eagles ran into a brick wall

Tom Crean looks on as Marquette plays Kansas in the 2003 Final Four.
*From the Marquette University Department of Special Collections and University Archives*

themselves known as the Kansas Jayhawks. In New Orleans, 54,432 fans at the Louisiana Superdome watched the birds from Lawrence, Kansas, pluck the Eagles from Milwaukee 94-61. The 33-point margin of victory was the second largest in Final Four history. The Jayhawks shot 53.5 percent against Marquette and controlled the boards, finishing with a 52-39 edge in rebounds. Five Jayhawks scored in double figures.

Marquette shot a season-low 31.1 percent from the field and only 18.8 percent from the three-point line. Wade led Marquette with 19 points, but he never had a huge impact in the game. Kansas's Kirk Hinrich and Michael Lee worked together to limit Wade's touches. Sophomore Travis Diener had one of the worse games in his college career as he shot one for 11 from the field and turned the ball over eight times. All afternoon the transition game of Kansas led to layups or dunks as the Jayhawks outscored Marquette 16-2 on fast-break points. Robert Jackson and Scott Merritt were not able to put together a strong interior game for Marquette, which would have helped to slow down the fast-paced Jayhawks.

Crean: "We missed so many close shots. It hurt our transition defense. Our big men were underneath the rim and they were not able to get back on defense. [The Jayhawks] were quicker on their break with getting down the floor on offense. We really made ourselves susceptible to easy baskets. If we would have made some of those shots around the rim while they were getting their transition defense setup, it was really a snowball. They played so well. They made shots. What we learned was we could never assimilate that break. Their break was so good. We couldn't put it out there where we could ever duplicate it."

This game was not indicative of the heart, courage, and dedication the Golden Eagles showed the Marquette faithful throughout the season. The team gave the university and their fans something to be proud of as they made a dramatic run to a place Marquette fans had not seen in many years—the Final Four. In the process they placed their names in NCAA and Marquette annals and showed the nation that Marquette basketball was back.

Crean: "I thought our guys continued to fight in that game and continued to go hard. I think we were shell-shocked much like Kentucky was a week earlier. Give Kansas credit, just like we deserve a lot of credit for the way we played against Kentucky. It wasn't as much as the way they played, as it was the way we played. I think that's what happened in the Kansas game. We missed some shots. It wasn't like we stopped working. Kansas just played so well. If they would have played even close to that well on Monday night, they would have been national champions. That's the way the game works; that's the way the game goes. Syracuse did it. Syracuse won the game."

# Players Transferring

Crean: "We gave him enormous opportunity. Dameon [Mason, who asked for his transfer in April 2005] had a chance everyday to be a better player, a better person, a better student. Hopefully, he took advantage of it in the years he was with us. I hope he finds what's working for him, but our team is moving on, as coaches we're moving on, recruiting-wise we're moving on. Anytime you go from being a high school hotshot and you want to be great, there's going to be some steps along the way.

"Sometimes, people around you don't allow you time to go through those steps. They can get inside of it. That's not any fun, either. There is a process. Dwyane Wade went through a process; Travis Diener went through a process. You name it, there's a process, and none of us can put a timetable on when that is going to take shape. I know that Dameon's a nice young man. We gave him every opportunity to be successful here in all areas of his life. I lay my head down at night knowing that, knowing that he was treated fairly and right—and put in a great atmosphere to be successful. He just chose to do something else. Like I said, I hope he finds what he's looking for.

"Anytime somebody's in a position to make a decision, you've got to evaluate those decisions all the time. We're not of the school, 'If it's not broken, don't fix it.' We are of the school, 'If it's not broken, let's fix it.' Let's keep figuring out what we can do to make it better. We've had some players come in here who did not want to put that effort into their schoolwork or the team. You know what? You owe it to everybody else in your program to make sure that you're holding everybody accountable to that. That's what we're trying to do. I think what happens is if you look around the country right now, there is such an instant gratification mindset throughout college sports and especially right now in college basketball.

"You just have to keep it in context. What's most important? Are they getting a great education? Are they doing the things that make the school proud? Are they working hard for each other, on the floor, in the weight room, all those things? As we add players, we've got to make sure that the star of the team is the team. Our media guides will have everybody on them; the posters will have everybody on them. We're not going to focus on the individual. That's how this program was built. That's how we're going to continue to build."

# CHAPTER 12

# Dwyane Wade

Coming out of Richards High School in Oak Lawn, Illinois, Dwyane Wade was not a highly recruited player. Coach Tom Crean saw immense potential in the six-foot-four guard, so he recruited Wade to join the Marquette basketball family. Wade entered Marquette as an NCAA partial qualifier in 2000 and was forced to sit out a year as he worked on his studies. Grateful for being given a chance at Marquette, Wade worked hard off of the court and joined the Golden Eagles for the 2001-2002 season. Eager to prove Marquette had made the right choice by taking a chance on him, Wade led the team in scoring, averaging 17.8 points, as the team earned its first trip to the NCAA Tournament since 1997.

During the 2002-2003 season, Wade took the Golden Eagles to heights they had not seen since 1977. Wade earned first-team All-America honors, was named the Conference USA Player of the Year, Conference USA Defensive Player of the Year, led Conference USA and was ranked 22nd nationally in scoring (21.5 ppg), and set a Marquette single-season scoring record with 710 points. The Golden Eagles won the Conference USA regular-season championship and earned the No. 3 seed in the Midwest Region of the 2003 NCAA Tournament. Wade and the Golden Eagles soared over the teams in the region, as Marquette beat Holy Cross,

Dwyane Wade dribbles around Kirk Hinrich during the 2003 Final Four.
*From the Marquette University Department of Special Collections and University Archives*

Missouri, Pittsburgh, and Kentucky to earn its first trip to the NCAA Final Four since 1977. In the victory over Kentucky that ended the Wildcats' 26-game winning streak, Wade registered Marquette's first triple-double since 1994 when he totaled 29 points, 11 rebounds, and 11 assists, and was the third-triple double in NCAA Tournament history.

In the spring of 2003, Wade decided to leave Marquette early and entered the NBA draft. He was selected fifth overall by the Miami Heat. Wade quickly became a superstar in the NBA as he helped to revitalize the Heat and to lead them back into the playoffs. In his second year, Wade and new acquisition Shaquille O'Neal took the Heat to within one game of the 2005 NBA Finals.

## Deciding to Go to Marquette

Wade: "The main thing coming out was that I wasn't highly recruited. They recruited me. They were saying the best things and offering the best things. It wasn't far from home. It was a program that was down and looking to be turned around. I thought that Coach Crean could really get it turned around, and I wanted to be part of it. It was an easy choice for me.

"I think he saw something in me that a lot of people didn't see. He thought I could get a lot better. I had things in me that you couldn't teach. That was toughness. He kept telling me I was going to get better. I don't know if I knew it, or he knew it, or anybody knew how good I was going to be or how soon I was going to be good. But we all knew in the long run it was going to work out, especially with the talent coming in and with the recruiting power that he had coming from Michigan State. He was going to get good players. He did a great job taking a diamond in the rough position."

## Sitting out a Year

Wade: "That was one of the most difficult things I have ever been through in my life. Anytime in life when something was going wrong for me, I always had basketball to turn to. I could go and play basketball, but my freshman year I didn't have basketball to turn to. I didn't have my teammates to turn to. I had to turn to my books. It was a hurtful time. I couldn't be out with my teammates after a win, and with a loss I thought it was all my fault.

"It was a tough and trying year, but it made me stronger. If I had it to do all over again, I would do it again, because it made me stronger. It made me a better player. And the next year I wanted to do anything I could to help my team win and to help myself get better and just to prove to people that the year was worth the wait. I was going to every game and hoping that all the fans and people at Marquette would be happy they let me come in as a Prop 48, a partial qualifier. To prove to them that I was worth the wait, that I was going to do right by Marquette and do well for the program."

## Something Special in 2002-2003

Wade: "Coming off my first year when we went to the tournament, we lost five players. We lost Odartey Blankson and some of our younger guys. But as we got into summer practice and we started playing together, we started thinking we had the right mix of guys. We didn't have the best team probably, but we had the right mix of guys on this team. We felt that if we could get it all together and everybody grew quickly, that we could do something special. And we did, that was one of the best teams that I ever played on because everybody knew their role. Guys wouldn't take shots, would take charges, would go for a rebound, or whatever. That was good. We needed that. I credit Coach for putting the right people around Travis and me to help us get to the Final Four. We had Steve Novak knocking down threes at 50 percent. We had Joe Chapman doing the same thing. Our young guys really did a great job. Rob Jackson playing that year really helped us a lot. He helped Scott Merritt a lot. We had a great team. We kind of knew we could do something special once we got to practice."

## The Superdome Picture

Wade: "There's nothing better as a player when you feel like your coach believes in you no matter what. You want to do it for them. When Coach Crean took us to the Superdome and told us we could be playing here, that meant a lot to all of us. That meant he had the confidence in us before anybody else did. He told us we'd be sitting there and playing there. It was great. We just had to have the confidence that we'd get to New Orleans.

"Every game he'd say, 'You signed this picture, then you've got to be in.'

"Everybody signed that picture; he made sure we weren't coming up short of our goal."

## Beating Kentucky

Wade: "The first thing I remember is warming up. We just looked down at the way Kentucky was warming up. They looked like they had the feeling, 'We are playing Marquette. Who are they?' And that just lit a fire under us. We saw they were not taking us seriously. We were one of the best teams in the Tournament, and we wanted to prove it. I just wanted to go out and do anything I could. If this was going to be my last game as a college basketball player, I was going to go out there and play as hard as I could. And we did. We played great in all facets of the game. From start to finish, everybody came in and did their job. It was the best game I ever played in college. I've played a couple in the NBA I thought were better, but it was the best I ever played in college.

"The whole week leading up to the game was great. We had unbelievable practices. Our team was unbelievably together. All we did was hang out with each other, saying, 'We're going to do this. We're going to do this. Nobody believes we're going to do this.' It was great. The memories of that time, of that moment, will live with all of us forever. Whatever the guys go on to be, doctors, governors, or whatever, the memories of that the Final Four run, the win versus Kentucky will always be there in the back of their heads."

Dwyane Wade celebrates after Marquette beat Kentucky in the 2003 NCAA Midwest Regional Finals.
*From the Marquette University Department of Special Collections and University Archives*

## Decision to Go Pro

Wade: "It was a little more difficult than people think. I can honestly say this, if I wasn't married with a child at the time, I probably would have stuck for my next year. I loved what we had at Marquette. It was tough. We worked hard, but I loved what we had. I loved what Coach made of Marquette, and I loved my teammates. I wanted to stay there the next year, but I had a responsibility to take care of. I really had to get outside of my box and say, 'I have to take care of my family. And this is the best way I can do it.' It was hard, being in college with a young son and a wife. It was an easy decision that way, but it was a hard decision because of the chemistry we had, the family that we were at Marquette."

## Prepared for the NBA

Wade: "I think I was overprepared because we practiced so hard at Marquette. Practice was way harder than the game. We practiced so hard every day, everything was structured, everything was kind of like it is in the NBA—the way Coach Crean treated us. Even though I was going to Miami, one of the toughest teams, toughest coaches, toughest training camps in the NBA, I thought that I was ready because in my heart and in my mind I couldn't do anything tougher than I could have at Marquette. To this day I haven't seen anything tougher. You get tired, but nothing has ever been tougher than Marquette. I can say Coach really prepared me. I think Travis [Diener] will see this year when he goes to Orlando that he is really overprepared for everything."

(Diener was drafted in the second round of the 2005 NBA draft.)

"Like we had a lot of plays at Marquette, there are a lot of plays in the NBA. He is going to pick them up fast, because he is used to it; our brains are trained like NBA players already. That's why I came in and had the solid impact my rookie year that I had. Because I already felt like I had done this before, I could do it again only on a higher level."

## Post-Marquette Relationship with Coach Crean

Wade: "We're still friends. He is still my coach. Anytime I have a bad game, anytime I have a good game, Coach is always calling me, giving me pointers. He is always sending me films—Marquette films. Whatever happens, he is sending me films of the way I used to play, the things I used to do. It helps me out so much because if I go through a stretch where I'm not making plays for my

Hard work during practices and games at Marquette helped to prepare Dwyane Wade for the NBA. *From the Marquette University Department of Special Collections and University Archives*

teammates, he'll send me a tape and say, 'Dwyane, this is the way you used to do it. Get back to doing it that way.' He's always going to be my coach. I respect him for it. Not a lot of people can tell me now in my life that I need to do this or I need to do that. There's not a lot of people who are willing to tell me that at this stage in my life because of the power that you have when you have money. Coach Crean is one of the people who keeps me down on earth. He is still my coach. I listen to what he says. We have a good friendship. He has kids; I have kids."

## Marquette in The Big East

Wade: "I know Coach will do the best that he can. I don't know if he'll get another Travis Diener or another Dwyane Wade, but I'm sure he can get some players who can play and take them to the next level.

"Travis is a unique player. I don't think a lot of people knew how unique Travis was for Marquette. Marquette will miss Travis.

"Coach will do a great job. The Big East is a bigger conference. More players are going to be attracted to go to Marquette if they want to get better, if they want to work hard. If they don't want to work hard, they are not going to go to Marquette. If they want to work hard and get better, they'll go there."

## Legacy of Leadership

Marquette welcomed Wade back to the Bradley Center and Al McGuire Court before its game against South Dakota State on December 7, 2004. Marquette president Father Robert Wild, athletic director Bill Cords, and Coach Crean presented Wade with the Dwyane Wade Legacy of Leadership Award. The award will be given out annually to the Marquette player who most exemplifies the traits displayed by Wade during his years at Marquette.

The second-year NBA star with the Miami Heat was in town to play a game against the Milwaukee Bucks the next evening. Several of Wade's teammates including NBA superstar Shaquille O'Neal and Miami Heat head coach Stan Van Gundy were present to see Wade honored by his college team. Wade enjoyed his time back at his alma mater as he delivered a pregame pep talk to the team and spent the game on Marquette's bench.

# Chapter 13

# Travis Diener

T ravis Diener earned the admiration of all Marquette fans with his leadership and hard play. The six-foot-one guard from Fond du Lac, Wisconsin, teamed up with Dwyane Wade to lead the Golden Eagles to the NCAA Final Four in 2003. His MU career was cut short during his senior year after he broke two fingers on his left hand. Diener, who was a mere 83 points from breaking Marquette's all-time scoring record, was forced to watch the final five games of his college career in street clothes. Diener's toughness and leadership were not overlooked by NBA scouts. He was drafted in the second round of the 2005 NBA draft by the Orlando Magic.

## Marquette Career

Diener: "I always pictured myself having a great career; my expectations for myself were really high. I've had a wonderful career here, the people have been great, and my teammates have been great. Most importantly, my coaches have believed in me and taught me the right way. I've really matured as a player and a person. My game has gotten that much better. I don't know, coming out of high school, if I ever thought I'd be in the position I am. But I'm thankful, and I'm just going to try to keep working as hard as I have and just try to take it to the next step when I get healthy again."

Travis Diener, Dwyane Wade, Tom Crean, Scott Merritt, and Robert Jackson (left to right) watch the closing moments of a Golden Eagles victory.
*From the Marquette University Department of Special Collections and University Archives*

## Bad Break

Diener: "It's hard to sit back and watch these guys practice, watch them play, knowing I'll never play again for Marquette. In the same breath, I know I still have to be here and encourage these guys and try to motivate them. Hopefully we can make a run in the last weeks of the season with the conference tournament and see what happens. Overall, I've had a pretty good attitude about it; I haven't really said, 'Why me?' It's not worth it; you just have to keep a positive attitude about it. That's what I've done for the most part."

## Tom Crean's Influence

Diener: "He's a guy who's been there for me my whole four years here, the things he's done for me when I've had tragedy [my brother died during my freshman year] and when I've had something go wrong for me. When I injured my hand, he was there constantly for me at the doctor's, getting opinions for me, trying to help any way that he could. He'd invite me out just to be with him. He's been like a father figure to me; you just can't find that in every coach. You'd be crazy to think that every college coach has the same relationship with his players. It's an intense program, but it's a lot of fun. If you like to play hard for a guy who's going to give extreme effort and intensity and energy to the program and the people whom he loves, then this place is a perfect fit, and that's what he's been to me.

"Obviously, I wanted to stay close to home, but there's a number of schools close to home that I could have chosen. He drew me with how he believed in the program, how he thought the program was going to evolve during my time there. There was a 15-14 season two years before I got here, so probably not many people believed we'd be in the Final Four two years after I got here. But every guy who played on the team that year believed that, and he sold it to us, and he was the main guy who made all that happen."

## Memories

Diener: "That's the goal of every basketball player, to try to be a winner. You try to make your team as good as possible. That Final Four year was something special that nobody can ever take from me, our team, or our coaching staff. There are so many great memories I've made here, the bonds I've made with my teammates, some of whom are my best friends. The bonds I've made with every coach who has coached me, and the fans, and the community here in Milwaukee. It's been unbelievable. I have no regrets. The year that we went to the Final Four was the most successful as a basketball player obviously, but every year I've been here at MU has been a blast. Win or lose, you try to win. We put it all on the court every

Dwyane Wade (left) and Travis Diener walk off the court during the 2003 Final Four.
*From the Marquette University Department of Special Collections and University Archives*

time we play. But I've had a lot of fun here. It's been a great honor to play for a program that has this much vision."

## Travis the Competitor

Diener: "I don't know where it comes from. It's just a desire to win. I think a lot of players have it; it comes out different ways. With me, it's just all-out hustle, just trying to do whatever. I try to vocalize for my teammates, to be loud, to encourage them, or get on them if they're not giving the effort. Sometimes, I think maybe I'm too hard on guys. But they know that my only goal is to win; I'm not out to have a personal problem with anybody. My teammates have been great. They want to win just as bad as I do. I don't know where it comes from. I was born with it; my family raised me that way. I've carried that my whole life."

## Preparing to Watch Senior Day

Diener: "I think it'll be extremely hard come Saturday, wearing street clothes like I am tonight, and not being able to play in front of our home fans for the last time in my career. It's difficult; it's been hard at times, during the Cincinnati game, during the course of the week not being able to practice. I've been constantly going to see doctors, and rehabbing, things like that. I don't know what emotions I'm going to have Saturday. I'm going to try to stay calm with everything and not get caught up with it. I want to try to be there to motivate my teammates; there's a bigger thing than Senior Day; that's to try to get that win."

## Connection with the Fans

Diener: "The fans ultimately make or break a program. You can win and feel good about yourself; you're going to share with your teammates and coaches, but the fans are what built this place. For the four years I've been here, they've been great. We've been in the top 10 or 15 in attendance [for schools in the country] every year I've been here. When you can have that home-court advantage the way we've had it my four years, it's hard for a visiting team to come here and win. I can't thank the fans enough for what they've brought to me. It's an honor to play in front of the people here in Milwaukee, the people here in Wisconsin, and I've always stayed loyal to whatever I've been committed to. I'll always stay committed to Marquette basketball and the state of Wisconsin in general as a basketball state."

## A Difficult Conclusion

As it turned out, Marquette could not win without Travis Diener. The 2004-2005 regular season ended on a sour note, with a home-court loss to St. Louis. The Golden Eagles then lost to TCU in the first round of the Conference USA Tournament.

They accepted a bid to the NIT, where they lost to Western Michigan.

# CHAPTER 14

# The Voices of Marquette

For 15 seasons, Steve "The Homer" True and George Thompson teamed up as the radio announcing pair for Marquette games broadcasted on WISN radio in Milwaukee. A native of South Bend, Indiana, True came to Milwaukee in 1989 to host a sports talk radio program on News/Talk 1130 WISN. During that year, Marquette was looking for a new play-by-play announcer to team with color analyst George Thompson. After a brilliant career at Marquette where he became the school's all-time leading scorer, Thompson entered the Marquette radio booth after a career in professional basketball. When True arrived, Thompson had already been serving as Marquette's color analyst for 12 years. Thompson retired from the broadcasting booth after the 2004-2005 season.

## Basketball in New York

Thompson: "Al [McGuire] had a contact in New York. In the five boroughs, back in those days, for like 15 cents, you could go to any of the boroughs on a train. So, wherever the action was—whether it was up in Harlem, out on Long Island, Brooklyn—it didn't matter. Guys would find out, and everybody would show up on Saturdays and Sundays. Everybody knew each other. Basketball, even now, is a really small community. In New York, everybody played against everybody. Billy Crystal used to play for Long Beach High. We went out and played them. I've seen Billy Crystal four or

George Thompson is the all-time leading scorer in Marquette basketball history with 1,773 points. *From the Marquette University Department of Special Collections and University Archives*

five times since then. He had a standup routine about me in the early days about playing basketball in New York. So everybody knew each other; everybody knew the McGuire brothers. Dick was good, and Al was not good, but he was entertaining! They came out. I didn't want to go to UCLA with Kareem, because that was a factory at that time. I was more interested in going to a school that had a good basketball tradition. But I wanted the chance to create another legacy, building upon what had already happened. When I went to Marquette, I knew Dean Meminger and Pat Smith, Butch Lee and all those guys. I mean we all played together for years so we had a leg up when they showed us campus. It wasn't, 'Hi, I'm George. I'm Dean.' It was, 'Hey, where's the party?!' Then Al was the salesman; Al would close the deal."

## More Head Than Body

Thompson: "Al really got in your face all the time and yelled at you a lot. He was still yelling at me on Monday after a Saturday game. He'd kick Pat Smith out of practice or suspend him four or five games a month, or whatever. In the end, Al became like part of the family. You don't get along with everybody in your family. For every good story I can tell you about Al, I could tell you another one that wasn't good. I guess you have to add it all up. There are more plusses in the column than minuses.

"Al had a way of coaching. He could come into a game without even seeing a scouting report. Hank Raymonds did a great job with all of that.

"Hank told me one night a guy I was guarding would always end up on a certain side of the floor. It was on the right-hand elbow side. [Hank] put an X there. I think the first five minutes we ran past and [Hank] was standing on it. The other time, he was right next to it.

"But Al didn't care about any of that. Al knew how to adjust. He knew when to go zone, play man-to-man, slow the ball down. When we got seven points up, we considered that hold-the-ball time. And they didn't have the shot clock then. But anywhere from seven to nine points was the magic number. I don't know if anybody's ever figured this out, but when Al McGuire's teams got up seven to nine points, the percentage of wins was probably in the high 90s. Because then it was not only physical, but psychological. We'd run a weave. We ran a weave for one game three and a half minutes and then ended up with a back-door layup. The crowd went crazy. Imagine what that does to your opponent? So Al was more about the head than the body, 'cuz he was a terrible basketball player.

"The only reason he played in the NBA was because his brother, Dick, was so great. [Al] was more about the head, and everything he had to say had to do with later on, after basketball.

"Al always said, 'Don't let basketball use you, use it.'

"If you look at the guys in the 10 or 11 years that he coached, there are probably in the high 80 or low 90 percentile—all of them are successful now. That's probably something that a lot of people don't get about Al."

## American Express

Thompson: "When I signed my first contract, he said to me, 'Now, George, you gotta establish your credit. Go out and get yourself an American Express card. And pay it off every month.'

"That's how he was. I've been an American Express cardholder since 1969. That gives me an idea for a commercial!"

## Getting Through

True: "I don't know that I got into [Al McGuire's] inner circle. His wife said that. Al was nice to everybody. He made everybody feel better. It was just a pleasure. He would entertain me. Every time I went there, I would always feel better after I saw him than before. He'd make you laugh; he'd say stuff. Everybody likes to be around somebody who makes them laugh or feel better. He was that one person.

"I don't presume to say that I knew him like a friend. I didn't know that much about him. I learned about him, but it was a real pleasure. In a selfish way, I couldn't do anything for Al. I could buy meals for him, but everybody did that. But it was always kind of one way. I miss it because he was fun to talk to. You just never knew what he was going to say. He made you laugh and feel good. I think he did that for a lot of people, that is never talked about as much as his antics and all the stuff he did; he was a great coach.

"The best thing about Al to me is also the way he got through to George Thompson and all the players of that era. It was the way they carried themselves. It's about being really good at basketball. But it's also about what they've done beyond that as to how they judge themselves and the program. I don't know if he saw that in the people when he recruited them. I suspect he probably did. Or that he was a part of making them that way. I suspect that when he recruited them and saw how they treated their parents, that was the key to knowing what they had."

## People Change

True: "When I grew up in South Bend, we thought Al McGuire was the anti-Christ! He was like the devil.

"I don't know when I first met him. It was just one of those special treats—somebody who entered your life. Al was doing the games; it wasn't that many years ago.

"I know this from my own father. I didn't see Al when he was younger. When you meet somebody when they're a little older, they're a different person. Somebody who meets my father now would have no clue to what he was like 10 or 20 years ago."

## Al 'Til the End

Thompson: "It was like losing a member of your family when Al died, especially when he tried to still be Al, and I had had a conversation with him a week or so before.

"He said, 'George, when the guys come, I gotta sit up.'
"I said, 'You don't have to sit up, why?'
"He said, 'I can't let 'em see me being weak.'

Steve "The Homer" True (right) and George Thompson (left) discuss the action on the Marquette hardwood. *From the Marquette University Department of Special Collections and University Archives*

"I said, 'Look, it is what it is right now.'

"He talked a little more, and he sat up and he said, 'Help me put my legs back up on the bed.'

"When we'd visit, he never tried to sit up after that. Guys would come in; the old guard would just kind of get out of the way and let the other guys talk to him. He never tried to do what he couldn't do anymore, because he had this thing in his head that he was still Al from, you know, the 1960s and 1970s. He kind of came to grips with that. In a funny sort of way, that was kind of me saying something back to him about life. That was like a lot of things he told me."

## Getting Teamed-up

True: "[George] didn't have any choice. Bob Dolan [the former Marquette announcer] actually did Marquette games for one year, and then he left. He didn't want to do a sports talk show [which came with the play-by-play]. So he left the station, and then they brought me in to do the games and a sports talk show. George had no say. We met the day of the game."

Thompson: "It was the night of the first game. We signed our contracts at the Hyatt about two hours before the first game."

True: "It was Kevin [O'Neill's] first game and the first exhibition game. Something tells me he lost that game."

Thompson: "All I know is it was a strange way to start out a relationship, to meet the guy you're going to be spending a whole lot of time with two hours before the first game. But in a weird kind of a way, it typifies what we've been doing ever since. The things you see on television now. These pregames things—with eight or nine guys there with funny suits trying to be really jovial and all that—we were doing that 14 years ago. And I don't think people really got that."

True: "We're just having fun. That's always been the standard. The thing that's different is George doesn't do it like a normal analyst who feels he has to comment on every play—like that's the focal point. It's always a stream of consciousness with both of us. It's just fun. Part of it may be chemistry. Part of it is people can tell when you're having fun. They can tell when both people are having fun, and when one's having fun and the other is not. It's just real easy."

Thompson: "The game part is easy, but getting there and dealing with all the other issues; that could give one cause. But the game part—if we could just be transported down into those seats a half an hour before the game, I could do this forever or as long as I live, whichever came first."

## Preparation Before Each Game

True: "Oh, I spend *tons* of time! *Hours and hours!* Sometimes, we're not at our best because we haven't slept—we've done so much preparation!"

Thompson: "I guess the best thing you can say about our relationship is that we hang out when we're not on the air. I think preparation is the most overrated thing that there is."

True: "George doesn't have to prepare; George knows basketball. To me, I don't want the analyst to tell me how tall somebody is or how many points they score. I want him to tell me what he's seeing, what's going on. It doesn't happen that much in basketball, but people can use stats and stuff like that just to fill versus 'This is what I'm watching and seeing. What are you watching and seeing?' That's the show. You want to make sure, from my end, that you're accurate with the names and stuff. But people don't remember that; they remember the feel of watching the game. I've said, 'No one's ever told us we called a great game when Marquette lost.' But when the team wins, 'Aw man, you guys were on fire!' We both claim we're both at our best when it's a 40-point blowout, because to us it's more than a game, so who knows what catches our attention. No one talks about the era of Bob Dukiet [a former MU coach]; you could have had Eddie Doucette [the former Bucks play-by-play announcer] doing the games, and people wouldn't have said, 'That was a great time.' To be here when Dwyane Wade was here was lucky. People say, 'George, you don't seem as excited as you were when Wade was here.' Duh! How could you be?"

Thompson: "We both do our own special thing. If you match a tape up of 'Homer' calling the game, he's accurate in the 99 percentile. I just fill around that about what's in the heads and why things happen and why referees do what they do. We can do different things, but it's in sync. I'm not trying to do a whole lot of numbers. Just when they're pertinent like when a team's getting out-rebounded by 10 or 15 rebounds. One team has 10 offensive rebounds that they put back for eight, 10, 12 points, that's a pretty good statistic. Turnover ratio—assists to turnovers, that's a very important statistic. Stuff like that I care about, because that has a real effect on the outcome of the game."

## Covering Dwyane Wade

True: "I thought he'd be good; I did not think he'd be this good [in the NBA] this fast. I've said, 'The best moment of the entire time that we've worked together was after the Kentucky game' when George said, 'He's the best who's ever played here.' It was just so special. You have to know George to know that he didn't say that just to say that. That, to me, was the defining moment that indicated just how good George thought he could be. He didn't say the best that was ever at Marquette. He said the best ever in terms of what he'd done and what he was going to do. You'd have to ask George to tell you what he saw, but that told me that he was going to be really good.

"As a rookie in the playoffs, Wade did in the NBA, what he did in Conference USA. You'd watch and say, 'Yep, that's what he did in college.' He just did everything and took over. From an announcing standpoint, it wasn't that he was just good, Dwyane was so entertaining. I'd say before a game, 'Okay, George, what's he going to do tonight that we haven't seen?' He was supposed to run out of things in two years, but he never did. From an entertainment standpoint, it was a once-in-a-lifetime thrill. I'm not saying there won't be another player to come around. But to have one play and entertain like he did, I'll be really surprised if I ever say, 'Hey, this is just as good as when Dwyane Wade was here.'"

Thompson: "I've seen some many really, really good guys who've played against us. 'Homer' says I played in the first Marquette–DePaul game, which was about 100 years ago! That was wrong! I played in 96 of 'em!

"When I first saw this guy, I told people, 'This is the best guy who ever played at Marquette.' Right away, everybody wanted to tell me that I was being falsely modest. I'm saying, 'Well, you asked me, and I gave you my opinion. You do whatever you want to do with it, but I'm tellin' you. I've seen this guy do some things that maybe Michael Jordan and Connie Hawkins have done.' I saw him do one thing I haven't seen anybody else do. He jumped up in the air, and went sideways. It was like he had a jet on one side like out of space! He jumped up in the air and went sideways. And I said, 'That's it. That's it.'

"At this point, where am I goin'? Who am I BS-ing? I graduated in 1969. Everybody talks about the scoring record now. I said, 'Travis Diener's had a heck of a career; he's a great ballplayer. He's got a heart bigger than he is. Whatever he gets, he deserves.' I believe that. Some people say, 'Yeah, you're just saying that.' But after 35 years, we've got some geeks at work that'll be searching to see if that's the longest string in Division I now. I'm saying, 'Hey, it could have happened before, but it didn't.' Now that there's a good possibility of it happening, so be it. I don't worry about things I have no control over, anyway. I certainly don't have any control over that. Everything goes in cycles. It's been a really long cycle for me, ya know?"

## Most Memorable Game

True: "The game I remember the most was the first time Marquette and Wisconsin played in the Kohl Center. They served Chinese food in the pregame! I've never, ever been anywhere where they've served Chinese food.

"But, aside from that on the court, yeah, the Kentucky game. The Louisville games, too, where Brian Wardle hit a shot and [Aaron] Hutchins hit a shot, those two games. When they beat Kentucky the first time [in the NCAA Tournament] when Kevin O'Neill was the coach. The Final Four thing was obviously bigger 'cuz that was to go to the Final Four. But that win under O'Neill was every bit as special, because it kind of validated that Marquette—if they weren't back, it was like, 'You know what? It's not like it was when Al was here, but we can be good. We can contend.' I don't think you ever forget the first game like that. But when you're going to the Final Four, and it's basically garbage time the last 10 minutes; it's like a parade. It started with 10 minutes to go. Who would ever have thought that? The process to get to the Final Four even though they got crushed; you can't take away what it felt like for all four of those games, getting [to New Orleans]. They were all great games; they were all tough games."

Thompson: "Plus, the food is better; the coverage is better; everybody's happier. The ham sandwiches are better; the beer is colder. Tony Miller basically took over that first Kentucky game [in the second round of the Southeast Region].

"He said, 'I refuse to be pressed by these people.'

"Not only did he beat the press; he got layups. That's how you beat the press. That's what he was doing. He just refused to be pressed. I don't know where Tony is now in Europe. But if he doesn't play another game, that's the game that he can always look back on.

"The second Kentucky game, for me, was really emotional, to see Marquette crush them like that. Because, back when I played, they were still having first- and second-round games at most teams' arenas. My junior year, we played in Lexington, and I had four fouls in 10 minutes. They crushed us. They beat us by 15 or 16. But it came back around full circle, and we met 'em in Madison. We were big underdogs. We weren't even worried about that game; we *knew* we were going to win it. And they got re-crushed. All of that came back to me, when Marquette did that and did it with such ease. It was emotional."

True: "And anytime they beat Cincinnati's a big game."

## MU to The Big East

True: "I think they've wanted to be there for a long time; I think they've always wanted to go. There's a connection back east for Marquette; there always has been. It's real simple: Get the players who are good enough and you can compete. Conference USA's been a great conference—especially the last two years with the teams up top—Cincinnati, Louisville, Memphis, Marquette, Charlotte. You can take those five and compete with any five atop any conference in the country, and it's been that way for the past four or five years. Now you have Syracuse, Connecticut, but if you've got the players, you can compete with anybody. There are [C-USA] teams that are capable of doing that. For as long as it exists, it'll be right there with the ACC at the top basketball conferences."

Thompson: "One of the reasons why Al quit was he was a master of timing, even to the point of—and sometimes I say this to 'Homer' in games—it's better to get a bad call early than late. Let them get all of those bad calls against you out of their systems early. Give them your opinion; get in their ears. Then you have a much better chance of getting a square deal—and maybe even getting a call here or there. Because referees are human beings, just like everybody else! The best thing that ever happened to Marquette was [during the 2004-2005 season] during the South Florida game when the ball hit the top of the backboard. Marquette got multiple calls the rest of the way. It was so obvious to me that that was going to happen, because they had blown a big call in that game. Now, that's not hurting their reputation; all that's doing is saying, 'Hey, we're going to be really watchful about what's happening on the other end now, because we potentially lost the game for that team.' Even if it's 50/50; that team's gonna get that call, especially at home.

"As far as The Big East, that's the reason why Al quit. He saw that coming. He had a pipeline from the East, starting with me, basically. You had all these big schools up and down the coast. I visited St. John's, Syracuse; I never did get around to going to Maryland. But if you want to get out of New York, you don't have to go to California. You can go to Syracuse, to Providence, to Connecticut, or wherever, and you could still have your contacts back home. Al was just basically fed up with the game from the standpoint of all the stuff a college coach had to do, besides coach the game. That's the reason why the pro game is so attractive to people. All you have to do is win; you don't have to deal with alumni, the administration. There are administrations in the pros spending hundreds of millions of dollars; all they want is results. They don't care how you get it. He had timing down to long, medium, and short term. He would never waste what he called 'wasting a jump' in a game. Early in the game, a referee makes a bad call. He didn't jump on 'em right away. [The ref] knew he had screwed up. Then when you did jump on 'em, it was twice as effective. He had a great understanding of human nature, which was his best asset as a coach. It wasn't Xs and Os and all of that; he knew what to do when and under what situation.

True: "I always felt it was about the players. When he didn't feel he could get the kind of players necessary to win, it wasn't, 'Well I don't want to coach anymore', but it was like, 'I have no interest in coaching with players who aren't as good as the players I'm goin' against.' He was always fascinated with coaches he thought enjoyed playing with inferior talent and making the team as good as they were. He was like, 'I never understood that; I don't see what the point is. The point is to have the best players. It's about the players!' So, it seemed pretty simple, once you don't have the best players. I'm sure coaching was real simple, 'cuz it wasn't real complicated! He wanted the best guy out on the court and in crunch time get him the ball. It's not like me drawing up a play; it's like putting that position player in a position to do what they do best. I'm not trying to make them better than they are.

"'George, get him the ball, set a screen do it; go do it.'

"I was always amazed that Al could talk forever. The first interview I did with him, I said, 'Next time, I'm just leaving the mike and getting something to eat!' He just never stopped, and yet, if you were to ask him about a basketball situation, no answer ever took longer than 10 seconds.

"One time, Marquette was playing man-to-man on the inbounds on a pickoff play.

"He said, 'Why do you have your best player running around through nine screens on an inbounds play? Let them get the ball inbounds; I'll give 'em a basket if I have to. I'm not killing my best player on an inbounds play!'"

Thompson: "We never played man-to-man on an inbounds play. We always played a 2-3 zone on an inbounds play. And they usually had to throw it over the top, out by the top of the key."

True: "Let him get it. In other words, 'I'm not wasting the energy of my best player.' Because he would do the same to them. 'If you're going to let me do that, I'll just get your guy tired.' George always says, 'If you can't stop a guy, make him play defense.' That'll stop him from scoring as much. Like I said, it's simple stuff. But it works when you've got the players! If you don't have the players, the guy's goin', 'Okay, go right ahead.'"

Thompson: "But he had good players, and then he had some mediocre players blended in, but he had a way of making those guys play better by how he approached them. It was also important to make sure those guys who were trying to fit into the program didn't let the program down. When he saw guys who were on the cusp of being good or not, those guys got as much attention as the guys who he knew were good and he had to womp upside the head every day, verbally, like me. By midseason, some weeks, I didn't practice more than two days a week, 'cuz I'd get thrown out of practice. We'd get into it.

"He's say, 'Just go away.'

"I'd say, 'See ya, break my heart.'"

True: "This is all secondhand to me, but they always said he had one star each year. But he didn't want five stars on the floor. He knew five stars on the floor didn't work. It was a blend and a mix that he obviously understood. But as I said, I can imagine the energy level was so much higher. George told me the first day, [coaches] are all nuts; just understand that. In his prime, the amount of energy he must have had. Knowing what he had when I met him 30 years later; he had to be as whacko as the rest of 'em!"

Thompson: "But whacko with a motive. He'd go off on the referee; there'd be a timeout. He'd go off on the referee. Maybe he'd get a technical.

"He'd come back to the huddle and say, 'That was just for show. We'll get that back later on in the game.'

"I'm serious! We'd look at the guy and say, 'This guy's really strange!'

"But sometime he'd go completely off. He was out there! But usually, it was calculated. But every coach, even coaches who coach Little League, they're not right. Coaches who coach teenagers, and their livelihood, their family depends on them being successful—who are still dealing with puberty and pizza and girls and beer and all that stuff—they're whacko. All of 'em are wound too tight. That was one of the reasons I never wanted to go into [coaching]. I never wanted to go through that. If I could be a pro coach and just have assistants do all that other stuff—evaluate talent, do the drafts, and coach the games—that would be fine. But there's too much attached to being a college coach. The NCAA rule book is *this* thick. They have a full-time person at every major university to interpret that book."

CHAPTER 15

# Jim Langenkamp

D r. Jim Langenkamp lettered in basketball at Marquette in 1967 and 1968 under coach Al McGuire. In 1980, he rejoined the team in a new capacity as team physician.

## Recruiting Mothers

Langenkamp: "Al McGuire recruited me in 1965 when I graduated from high school. I think he recruited me because he needed a white guy from the state. It was different back then. Al didn't feel he could have everybody he wanted. There are more good players in five square blocks in Chicago then there are white kids in the state of Wisconsin. There was some pressure back then; it was different. I think he thought he needed one white kid from the state. He wanted me or the kid who went to Wisconsin and played at Marquette High. I can't think of his name. I was an All-State player from Wisconsin, a marginal Division I player. The thing about Al was he came up and told my mother I was going to go to Minnesota or Northwestern. He always recruited the mothers. I wasn't even Catholic. I was from Merrill, Wisconsin, up north. I got home, and my mother said, 'Jim, you're going to Marquette.'"

## Adolph Rupp's TV Show

Langenkamp: "In 1967, we went down to Kentucky and lost to Adolph Rupp. Al got into a contest with Rupp. We were playing Bowling Green.

"Adolph Rupp called Al and said, 'Son, I'd like you to be on my TV show. I always have a TV show.'

"Al said, 'Fine, my appearance fee is 7,000 bucks.'

"He said, 'Well son, we don't pay people to come on my TV show.'

"Al said, 'Well, then I won't be there. Bye.'"

## Demanding 100 Percent

Langenkamp: "Al didn't like the establishment. He recruited some players when I was there whom nobody else would recruit. There might be a problem. Al had a knack of getting 100 percent out of every kid. He didn't treat every kid the same. We had a kid name Brad Luchini from West Allis. He was a great player, but he was too white-bread for Al. He was his whipping boy. My roommate was Ed Smith from Harlem, whom any other coach in the country probably would have sent packing. But Al somehow got that kid to perform for him and got him a degree, which is amazing."

## Reading People

Langenkamp: "Al was from New York. He could read people. He could read refs. He could read coaches. He had a great sense of living in the present and what to do—work this ref, say one thing to this kid, do this with another kid. He was just great at reading people."

## Using Basketball

Langenkamp: "Al always said to his players, 'Use basketball. Don't let basketball use you.' He never had a lot of rules. He just expected you to show up and play. He expected you to go to class.

He had a great knack. One of the worst days of my life was sophomore year when grades came out and the team wasn't doing very well academically. I was in pre-med, and I wanted to get into med school. I had a 3.7 or 3.8.

"Al dragged me up in front of the team and looked around at the team and said, 'What the **** is wrong with you guys? Look at this kid, he comes to practice same as you. He got a 3.8. What the ****, you don't go to class?' He was yelling at Jackie Burke from New Jersey, whose father was a dock worker. He says, 'Jackie, you can either go to class or you can start shaping up on the docks like your dad did.'

"That was the worst practice of my life. I got the s— kicked out of me. First time down the court, I caught an elbow in the throat.

"He says, 'How's that smart boy?'

"Al wanted these kids to graduate. He wanted them to use basketball. Not just be used and thrown away. He wasn't like Bob Huggins, who takes kids, uses them for a couple years, and then they're out. Al wasn't like that. When Al recruited kids, he used to say, 'You have a full four-year scholarship: books, board, tuition, $15 a month laundry money. No matter what happens, that's what you got. And what I expect in return is that you show up and play and go to class.'"

## "How's Your Achilles?"

Langenkamp: "I operated on Al. I was in the training room seeing some athletes with David Lee, the trainer. I got a call from some cowboy orthopedist in Las Vegas.

"The orthopedist said, 'I got Al here. He just stepped off a stage here; he was interviewing some All-Americans here in Las Vegas. He tore his Achilles tendon.'

"Al was always so faithful to his ex-players.

"He said, 'I want to go back to Milwaukee and have Jimmy take care of it.'

Al McGuire tore his Achilles tendon in Las Vegas as he was headed to a speaking engagement. Dr. Langenkamp operated on McGuire in Milwaukee to repair the tendon (after Al completed his speaking engagement).

*From the Marquette University Department of Special Collections and University Archives*

"But first he went to San Francisco to give a talk, because they were giving him $6,000. He took the red-eye back to Milwaukee and showed up on Sunday at 5 a.m. He looked like shit, but he wanted that $6,000. I operated on him on Sunday. I fixed his Achilles. He never took any pain medication. I finally had to have the nurse put a sign on his door, no visitors. He needed some rest. He slept for 24 hours and went home. I told him to come back. He came back once, and I took his sutures out. I told him to come back to do rehab and I never saw him again.

"Five or six years later, I saw him at the Bradley Center doing a game.

"I said, 'Hey, Coach.'

"He said, 'Jimmy, Jimmy, how you doing?'

"I replied, 'How's your Achilles?'

"He asked, 'What?'

"I asked again, 'How's your Achilles?'

"He said, 'Oh, yeah, I forgot about that. I guess it's fine.'"

# CHAPTER 16

# Bill Cords

**B**ill Cords joined the Marquette family in 1987 after he accepted the position of director of athletics at Marquette. During his tenure, Marquette moved from independent status to the Midwestern Collegiate Conference (MCC) in 1988-1989, a charter membership in the very successful and widely respected Great Midwest Conference from 1990 to 1995, a charter membership in the nationally prominent and prestigious Conference USA from 1995 to 2005, and a membership in The Big East Conference. Attendance at men's basketball games continues to rank nationally (21st in 2001-2002, 11th in 2002-2003, and 12th in 2003-2004).

## Coming to Marquette

Cords: "When I interviewed, the only thing I knew about Marquette was Al McGuire and the NCAA championship. When I got here I was pleasantly surprised. I expected a campus of streets and buildings; what I found was an inner campus that was very pleasant. Once you got inside the campus, you didn't realize that you were in the middle of the city. The second thing was as I interviewed, I knew that there was difficulty in the basketball program. What I found was Marquette had tradition, great support, and it had won a national championship. That's what tradition is made of. At one point, they dominated college basketball. Outside of UCLA, they were the dominant force in college basketball during the Al McGuire years. Those are things that a lot of people want to build, and that Marquette already had. The second thing was the administration was very clear about what the athletics program needed to do. That was to move to the Bradley Center. Whoever came in needed to move men's basketball back to the level of national prominence. They wanted to have a strong broad-based program. They wanted a program that everybody could be proud of. At the time, we really couldn't beat many people in just about anything. That was their commitment; they were committed to supporting those goals. The people that I met with were outstanding. I learned a long time ago that you can have buildings and facilities, you can have big budgets, but if you don't have really good people to work with and to work for, then none of that will matter. I realized that the strength of this university was its people, and I was talking to them. I came because of the people, I came because of the goals that the university had and the challenges that they had laid out, and they were willing to support that."

## Finding a Head Coach

Cords: "Sometimes the situation is different because we've had three coaches here [in the Cords era]. Primarily when we first started—when we were replacing Bob Dukiet—we were looking for a coach, an assistant coach, an associate coach, from a top-10 program. If that's where we aspired to go with our program, we needed to have someone who knew all the things that it took to get there. Recruiting was a critical part of that."

## Kevin O'Neill Leaving

Cords: "Kevin [O'Neill] was clear to us. We had asked him to bring this program back to a level of prominence. He agreed that he would do that. We offered him a multiyear contract. We'd had discussions about how long he would stay here. His aspirations were that he had a responsibility here, a commitment here, and he would do what we asked of him. You can never know what's coming in the future. Institutionally, we knew that if he were successful, people would be coming after him. He knew that, too. So, when we got to the Sweet 16 [in 1994], we knew that people would come after him. Tennessee was one of them. Vanderbilt came after him the year before; he hadn't interviewed, but he turned it down. When he decided to leave, the one thing that we all agreed on was that he had done exactly what we asked him to do. We wished he would have stayed, but we understood why he left. It wasn't a shock and it wasn't a surprise. It works two ways; when you become very successful, you know that you'll be in demand; on the other hand, you would hope that success would make people want to stay. At the same time, Tennessee made a pretty good offer. That was not an easy decision [for him]."

## The Arrival of Mike Deane

Cords: "Kevin had done such a good job of building the program up, that we had established ourselves. We had good players in the program. At that point, you would believe that we had brought the program back to a point where we were looking for a head coach who had successful experience. It wasn't the best time because we were already into the Final Four. A lot of coaches who might have been available weren't available; they had already taken other jobs. So we put together what we thought was a good pool. We basically were looking for a head coach who had successful experience, because we felt that's what we needed in the program at that time.

"Mike fit that description. He had been at a major program [as an assistant at Michigan State]. Then he was a successful head coach at Siena. Mike came in, and he did a good job for us. The difficulty was that when he came in, we had a Sweet 16 program. Over the years we had success—but less of it. From the Sweet 16, we went to the finals of the NIT. Kevin predicted this. When he left he said, 'I'll tell you, you're probably going to end up in the NIT [because Deane lost three key seniors, Jim McIlvaine, Damon Key, and Robb Logterman], deep in the NIT, but I don't think you're going to be able to make a run in the NCAA Tournament.' After that, he said, 'I really don't know.' So we ended up in the finals of the NIT and we ended up in the second round of the NCAAs, getting upset by Arkansas—or we'd have been back in the Sweet 16 again. The next year, we were in the first round of the NCAA; that's when we played Providence. The next year, we got to the third round of the NIT. The last year we didn't go anywhere. That's about all I can say. I do want to say that Mike Deane came in, and he did a good job for us."

## Advice from Al

Cords: "When I first was on the search for a replacement for Bob Dukiet, I called [Al McGuire] and asked for his advice.

"He said, 'Always remember one thing. Head coaches have a job.'

"That's all he said. But, what he was saying is you may have to talk a head coach into taking a job; and it may or may not work. That's been difficult for programs that go after a head coach. All of a sudden, that coach decides that he doesn't want to go. That kind of puts things into perspective with regard to their program and your program. That's always a danger that you have to look out for. I never forgot that. We had people in that we had contacted who were head coaches; we had people who were top assistants. The thing that worked for us is that Michigan State played here in the first and second rounds [of the NCAA Tournament in 1999]. One of the keys to that was Tom Izzo. They were favored to go to the Final Four; there was a lot of pressure on them to go to the Final Four; sometimes the head coach won't allow his assistants to talk to anybody until after everything's done. I called [Izzo] and asked for permission to talk to [Tom Crean]. He was fine. He did things to help Tom. He wanted Tom to get a good job. He felt that this was a very good job opportunity for Tom."

# Meet My Wife

Cords: "When [Michigan State] came to play, I interviewed him in between the first and second rounds at the Hyatt. It was a clandestine meeting, of course, at 3 p.m. between games. We had agreed to go to a certain room. So I got to the room, and I was starting to open the door, and there's Tom. It surprised me a little bit, but Joani [Tom's wife] was with him. It was very clear to me that this was a tandem here. She came because it was important for her to meet me, as well as Tom. I was impressed with that. We went inside, and I talked to Tom for two hours. If you've ever talked to Tom, block a long time. Tom Crean, like Al, has the ability to take very complex ideas and concepts and reduce them to a phrase or sentence. When you go through an interview [with him] in two hours, you cover a lot of territory. After the first hour, it was very, very clear to me that this was exactly the person we were looking for in our program—in terms of his philosophy of basketball, in terms of his philosophy on life, values that he carried to both areas, and relationships.

"From that point on, it was a situation where I think Tom was really very interested. But he didn't want us to know that, and we were really very interested, but we didn't necessarily want him to know that. At the same time, it was like magnets being attracted. The process went on through the regionals through to the Final Four. Immediately after the Final Four, we offered him the job. Father Wild and I had gone and talked to him in East Lansing prior to the Final Four, because they were getting ready to go. After his return, he and Joani and Megan [Tom's daughter] came over to the news conference."

# Where It Starts

Cords: "I will never forget the morning paper [*Milwaukee Journal Sentinel*] the day after the news conference. We had gone out to dinner that night. I got up in the morning. Tom had to go back. He was on a radio show. I came by and picked up Megan and

Joani at the hotel. I hadn't seen the newspaper yet so I picked it up while I was waiting for them to come down to the lobby. It was a half-page color picture of Megan and Tom sitting on the podium waiting to talk. She was on his left. He had his left hand on the arm of her chair. She had her right hand on his left hand, and her head resting on his hand, looking. It was one of the neatest things I've ever seen! So I bought about 10 papers and gave them to Joani because that was special. That's the way it starts."

## Commitment

Cords: "I think Tom Crean is basically about two things. He's about commitments, and he is about relationships. Money has never been—and I don't think will ever be—an issue with him. What is important to him is commitment and relationships. As we became more successful, it was very clear to some "local pundits" who had labeled [the Marquette job] as a steppingstone. At the time, Tom and I had an understanding, as I had with other coaches. If somebody contacted me about wanting to talk to Tom, I would go talk to Tom. Or if somebody contacted Tom, he would let me know, and we would talk about it. That's how we did things. There were people who called and either contacted me or him, but he was not interested. That started after his first year, so it wasn't like these other things were new. That's an important part of it, but I think what Tom saw here, especially with the McGuire Center coming, was commitment. He was told when he came to Marquette that we were going to have a practice facility. He could see that commitment had been made. He saw the commitment on the part of the university and on the part of our fans.

"I'll never forget this. We played Dayton. He walked out on the floor, and he looked up at the stands, and it was almost full of Marquette students with gold shirts. That meant as much or more to him than just about anything you might want to do for him.

"He saw that, and he developed a great relationship with our students. He established great relationships in Milwaukee. It's all about relationships and commitment. He saw that here, and he felt that he had an opportunity to make things work here. And he is. I think that speaks volumes."

# Celebrate the Variety of Wisconsin and American Sport in These Other Releases from Sports Publishing!

**In Life, First You Kick Ass:
Reflections on the 1985 Bears
and Wisdom from Da Coach**
by Mike Ditka with Rick Telander
• 6 x 9 hardcover • 192 pages
• photos throughout plus an eight-page
  color-photo section
• $24.95

**Al McGuire:
The Colorful Warrior**
by Roger Jaynes
• 6 x 9 hardcover
• 275 pages
• eight-page photo insert
• $24.95

**Tales from the Wisconsin
Badgers**
by Justin Doherty
• 5.5 x 8.25 hardcover
• 192 pages
• photos throughout
• $19.95
• 2005 release!

**Riding with the Blue Moth**
by Bill Hancock
• 6 x 9 hardcover
• 252 pages
• photos throughout
• $24.95
• 2005 release!

**Game of My Life: Memorable
Stories of Packers Football**
by Chuck Carlson
• 6 x 9 hardcover
• 250 pages
• photos throughout
• $24.95

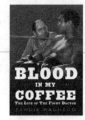

Jerry Tarkanian: Runnin' Rebel
by Jerry Tarkanian with Dan Wetzel
6 x 9 hardcover, 194 pages, eight-page
photo insert
$24.95
2005 release!

**Tales from the Packers
Sidelines**
by Chuck Carlson
• 5.5 x 8.25 hardcover
• 200 pages
• photos throughout
• $19.95

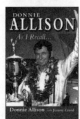

Dennis Rodman: I Should Be Dead By
Now
by Dennis Rodman with Jack Isenhour
6 x 9 hardcover, 300 pages, 16-page
photo insert
$24.95
2005 release!

**Reggie White: A Celebration
of Life**
by Sports Publishing L.L.C.
• 8.5 x 11 trade paper
• 128 pages
• color photos throughout
• $14.95
• 2005 release!

**Riddell Presents:
The Gridiron's Greatest
Quarterbacks**
by Jonathan Rand
• 8.5 x 11 hardcover
• 140 pages
• color photos throughout
• $24.95

*All books are available in bookstores everywhere!*
Order 24-hours-a-day by calling toll-free **1-877-424-BOOK (2665)**.
Also order online at **www.SportsPublishingLLC.com**.